AN INCOMPLETE GUIDE TO THE FUTURE

Icarus Lilienthal II by Hans Erni

An Incomplete Guide to the Future

WILLIS W. HARMAN

The Portable Stanford Series

SAN FRANCISCO BOOK COMPANY, INC.

San Francisco 1976

Library of Congress Cataloging in Publication Data

Harman, Willis W.
   An incomplete guide to the future.

   (The Portable Stanford)
   Bibliography
   Includes index.
   1. Economic forecasting. 2. Forecasting. I. Title.
HB3730.H318   1976b   338.5'443   76-26076
ISBN 0-913374-46-6
ISBN 0-913374-47-4 pbk.

Simon and Schuster Order Number 22376 (cloth); 22377 (paper)

Trade distribution by Simon and Schuster
A Gulf + Western Company

Printed in the United States of America

10 9 8 7 6 5 4 3 2 1

This book was published originally as a part of THE PORTABLE STANFORD, a series of books published by the Stanford Alumni Association, Stanford, California. This edition published by arrangement with the Stanford Alumni Association.

To Alfred M. Hubbard, who offered to the world what it was too foolish to accept, and to W. Dean Harman, whose generation must start the rebuilding.

CONTENTS

CREDITS

PAGE ii   Erni, Hans. *Icarus Lilienthal II.* 1941. Tempera. 150 x 187 cm. Sammlung Kunstmuseum, Lucerne. Courtesy Hans Erni, Lucerne.

PAGE 8   Rembrandt. *The Magician.* c.1632. Etching. Used by J.H. Lips as frontispiece to Goethe's *Faust,* Leipzig, 1790. British Museum, London.

PAGE 16   Dürer, Albrecht. *The Opening of the Fifth and Sixth Seals.* Woodcut. 395 × 285 mm. German edition of 1498. The Art Institute of Chicago. Potter Palmer Collection.

PAGE 20   Dali, Salvador. *Geopoliticus Child Watching the Birth of a New Man.* 1943. Reynolds–Morse Collection, Cleveland, Ohio. © by A.D.A.G.P., Paris, 1973.

PAGES 30–31   Erni, Hans. *Ut Omnia Exsolvantur.* 1964. Mosaic. 310 cm. Detail. Verwaltungsgebäude der Schweizerischen Radio– und Fernsehgesellschaft, Bern. Courtesy Hans Erni.

PAGE 36   Erni, Hans. *Gymnasion.* 1947. Tempera. 11¾" x 5⅞". Meyer & Thiessing, Zurich. Courtesy Hans Erni.

PAGE 38   "Excuse me, sir. I am prepared to make you a rather attractive offer for your square." Drawing by Weber. © 1971, The New Yorker Magazine, Inc.

PAGE 50   Seiwert, F. W. *Working Men.* 1925. Kunstmuseum der Stadt, Düsseldorf.

PAGE 57   Benton, Thomas Hart. *The Changing West.* 1930–31. Egg tempera and distemper on linen mounted on panel, 7'7" × 8'8". New School for Social Research, New York.

PAGE 66   Barlach, Ernst. *Hooded Beggarwoman.* 1919. Private Collection.

PAGE 73   Benton, Thomas Hart. *Wheat.* 1967. Acrylic on panel, 19¼" x 18¼". Courtesy Mr. and Mrs. R.H. McDonnell, Kansas City.

PAGE 78   Zeller, Magnus. *The Hitler State.* 1937. Märkisches Museum, East Berlin.

PAGE 88   Blake, William. *The Ancient of Days.* 1827. Colored print. 9³/₁₆" × 6⅝". Whitworth Institute, University of Manchester, Manchester.

PAGE 99   Erni, Hans. *O Waste of Loss.* 1942. Tempera. Verlag Ernst Scheidegger, Zurich. Private Collection. Courtesy Hans Erni.

PAGE 108   The Great Seal of the United States.

PAGE 112   Benton, Thomas Hart. *Instruments of Power.* 1930–31. Egg tempera and distemper on linen mounted on panel, 7'7" × 13'4". New School for Social Research, New York.

PAGE 127   Erni, Hans. *Planning and Realization.* 1943. Tempera. 36 x 33 cm. Art. Inst. Orell Füssli AG, Zurich. Courtesy Hans Erni.

PAGE 134   Dali, Salvador. *Metamorphosis of Narcissus.* 1936–37. Edward James Foundation. © by A.D.A.G.P., Paris, 1973.

PAGE 145   Erni, Hans. *Primitive Community.* 1943. Tempera. 40⅛" x 28¼". Meyer & Thiessing, Zurich. Courtesy Hans Erni.

Figures throughout the book are by Jim M'Guinness, Stanford. Special thanks to Sam Moffatt for his valuable assistance.

When I was in high school there were a number of puzzles going the rounds, and I remember one particularly. You were shown a network of railroad tracks and it was explained that a certain remote section of track had to be used by an eastbound train and then, a half hour later, by a westbound train. A switchman had the job of throwing a switch after the passage of the first train so that the way would be clear for the second. On this particular occasion the first train was late, and the switchman could see that the two trains were going to arrive at the crucial section of track at the same time. The telegraph wire was down and there was no way either train could be signaled to stop. What did the switchman do? After a suitable length of time you were supposed to give up, and be furnished the answer: He brought out a chair from the shack where he lived with his aging mother and set it on a knoll from which there was a good view of the track. Then he put her in the chair, saying, "You just set there, and in about ten minutes you're going to see the goldangedest train wreck you ever heard of."

Sometimes I feel like that. Since I began work in futures research, in 1967, it has seemed clearer and clearer to me that industrialized society in particular and the world in general are headed for a climacteric which may well be one of the most fateful in the history of civilizations. This convulsion is now not far off, and most people sense something of it—although interpretations vary widely, like the well-known interpretations of the elephant by blindfolded people who feel different parts of the animal.

I have tried to suggest a pattern for ordering contemporary events. You can't tell what's going on without a program, the saying goes; the program is what we seek. However, a pattern or an interpretation cannot be proven. You see the Gestalt or you don't; it appears plausible and useful or it doesn't. Thus I make no claim to authority or indisputability of argument. The point is not to agree or disagree—it is to observe together. If as the future unfolds the interpretation provided here seems to fit, then we have a useful guide to future action. If events belie the interpretation, then together we must seek another.

Several aspects of my life are pertinent to explain how the subject of this book became my dominating passion. My formal education was technical, culminating in the MS in physics and the PhD in electrical engineering from Stanford University in 1948. Between undergraduate and graduate work I was on active duty as a naval reserve officer for five years spanning World War II, the last military conflict engaged in by this nation in which it seemed clear to the participants what we were fighting for. I taught electronics, communication theory, and systems analysis at the University of Florida, the Royal Technical University in Copenhagen, and Stanford. Along the way I wrote several textbooks. Starting in 1967, by which time I was a professor of engineering-economic systems at Stanford, I began to be involved with the new discipline of futures research at Stanford Research Institute. This book is a summary of what I learned there.

But all of that, if not irrelevant, seems subjectively less important than several other landmark events. In 1954, at the age of 36, I was beguiled into attending a two-week summer seminar which I now recognize was a prototype of what later came to be known by such names as sensitivity training and the human-potential movement. I came away from that with a wholly new sense of the centrality of the task of self-discovery; from that point on my educational efforts took on a different focus.

Shortly afterward, in 1956, I encountered and was greatly influenced by the pioneering efforts of Alfred M. Hubbard, Humphry Osmond, Aldous Huxley, Gerald Heard, and others to institute a systematic study of consciousness, aided by such new tools as the psychedelic chemicals and biofeedback, and to give this new understanding an important role in the steering of society. Their attempt to bring this knowledge to the direct attention of world political and intellectual leaders was audacious and inspiring; if it appeared to fail, that was partly because of its being decades ahead of its time.

Finally, I think it significant to mention that somewhere around age 55 I discovered that I had a terminal illness—the one we somewhat euphemistically call aging. I could feel, and knew with unshakable intuitive understanding, that slowly and inexorably my body was making the decision to start to die. I find it difficult to describe exactly why this realization had such emotional impact, and even more difficult to explain why it was so edifying. It seemed to bring a kind of composure and nonattachment which contributes to the ability to be objective and nondistorting as one views the changing world. I expect to live at least another 20 years, and look forward to the further loosening of creature ties and the correspondingly improving clarity of vision.

A writer tells his readers about the world as he observes it. His perception, we all recognize, is affected by his specialized knowledge, the connoisseurship he has developed, the observing skills in which he has had formal training. But it is equally affected by the sorts of subjectively important events I have mentioned above; that is why they are relevant here.

I would like to acknowledge what I have gained from friends and colleagues, particularly those who worked on the SRI study, *Changing Images of Man*, and those at the Charles F. Kettering Foundation who kept faith. Cynthia Fry Gunn, Portable Stanford editor, were it not for her insistence to the contrary, would be accurately listed as co-author.

Willis W. Harman

Stanford, California
June 1976

INTRODUCTION

WE ARE ALL ACCUSTOMED to thinking of the past as a cause of subsequent events—a decision was made, a law was passed, an encounter took place, and *as a result* various other events transpired. We reason this way every day. Less obvious is the fact that our view of the future shapes the kind of decisions we make in the present. Someone has a vision of the future—of a great bridge, a new industrial process, or a utopian state—and *as a result* certain events are taking place in the present. Our view of the future affects the present as surely as do our impressions of the past or the more tangible residues of past actions.

This book entreats you to think about the future and, more importantly, to explore how our vision of the future affects the crucial decisions of today. Every action involves some view of the future—as we expect it to be, or as we desire it to be, or as we fear it may be. If our image of the future were different, the decision of today would be different. If our expectations are inaccurate, our decisions are likely to be faulty. If our vision is inspiring, it will impel us to action. If our collective vision arouses no enthusiasm, or if there is no commonly held image of what is worth striving for, our society will lack both motivation and direction.

We often assume (with considerable justification) that the most probable future is a direct continuation of past trends. Yet it is apparent today that many long-standing trends cannot continue unaltered: World population cannot forever expand exponentially; world energy use cannot increase endlessly; patterns of world mineral consumption must change. In fact, it has been apparent for several decades that modern society has broken with the past in a number of important respects. Peter Drucker has called our time "the age of discontinuity." In his book of that name, published in 1968, he described four important discontinuities with the past:

1. Genuinely new technologies, such as computers and semiconductors, were creating new major industries and rendering existing industries obsolete. Future technologies were most likely to stem, not from independent inventors, but from new knowledge of atomic and nuclear structure, biochemistry, psychology, and symbolic logic.

2. Major changes were taking place in the world's economy, moving it toward a worldwide economy and what Drucker calls "a global shopping center."

3. A new pluralist social and political organization was emerging in which all major tasks, from investment advising and care of the aging to dating and partygiving, were becoming institutionalized so that society was coming to be dominated by a web of overlapping, interdependent, special-purpose organizations.

4. Access to knowledge, rather than raw materials and transportation, had already become the crucial resource of modern economies. It was the major determinant of success in industries, represented the crucial capital, and was changing the character of work, the labor force, and education.

Drucker's book quickly became obsolete because new discontinuities have appeared that are at least as significant as the ones he had identified. It will suffice to mention five:

1. Individuals and governments alike began to recognize the serious threat from industrialized civilization to sufficiency of fossil fuels, minerals, and natural fresh water; of arable land and habitable space; of the waste-absorbing capacity of the environment; and of the resilience of the planet's life-support systems. This "new scarcity" was different in kind from the scarcities of food and shelter that have always been a part of human existence, being more fundamentally linked to approaching planetary limits.

2. Great masses of people were no longer content with the economic and political status quo. Rising levels of education and awareness, in part due to the impact of modern communications, had led to expectations of better living conditions and increased self-determination and had created dissatisfaction with the disparities and inequities of the old order.

3. Growing numbers of people in the industrialized nations had become disillusioned with the once-accepted belief that ever-increasing material growth and ever-expanding technology and industrialization would overcome world poverty and help mankind to achieve a more meaningful existence.

4. Nonindustrialized Third World nations began to exert new power. They became a moral force, influenced world economy by forming cartels of resource-producing nations, and demonstrated the disruptive capability of the discontented poor.

5. A "new transcendentalism" emerged, both in the general population and among a faction of scientists, which placed new emphasis on intuitive and spiritual experience. This new weight given to spiritual intuition reversed a long-standing trend toward empirical explanations and materialistic values.

Yet even this expanded list fails to capture the full spirit of our times. Significant as these discontinuities are, they appear to be manifestations of a far more fundamental change—a change involving all our social, political, and economic institutions; our social roles and expectations; and even the basic premises underlying modern culture and values. This change is not just an evolutionary development from one phase of history to another. Rather, the evidence suggests that the technologically advanced nations of the world may be approaching one of the great transformations of human history.

From a broad historical perspective, the modern industrial era is a brief episode—a jump from a preindustrial society in which man made relatively low demands on natural resources and had little impact on the natural environment to a "transindustrial" society in which man has a high ability to manipulate and shape his physical environment. Whereas industrial society's emphasis has been on economic and material growth, the transindustrial society would place more emphasis on human growth and development. Whereas industrial society has been greatly concerned with the physical frontiers of geography and technology, in the transindustrial society concern would shift to the inner frontiers of mind and spirit. In the transindustrial society institutions would have to serve persons, not the reverse. Learning would be a prime concern at all phases of life and of all social institutions—not an activity of limited duration in preparation for the "real" business of fitting into the institutions of the industrial state.

We tend to view recent decades from the perspective of our own lifespan. Thus we are impressed with the technological accomplishment and the seemingly endless cornucopia of physical products of modern industry. But taking the longer perspective, we can see the nature of the brief historical interval—this "jump" from preindustrial to trans-industrial society—that our industrial era comprises. Consider population growth for example. We have come to accept that the planet's population is increasing at about 2 percent per year, following an exponential growth curve. Yet in the longer historical perspective, from say 6000 B.C. to A.D. 6000, the plot of world population has to look something like the upper step curve of *Figure 1*. To grasp the significance of the metamorphosis to a transindustrial era, imagine a similar plot of the average demand that each individual makes on the environment through resources used and waste products discarded. Of necessity, this is an assumed arbitrary scale because appropriate data do not exist, but we can judge that the plot has to look something like the lower curve of *Figure 1*. Our present point in history is unique—illustrated both in terms of population growth and individual demands upon the environment: At no other time has such growth been so rapid. Because of planetary limitations, this exponential growth cannot continue; at some point it must once again level off.

Let me emphasize, however, that this future transformation to a transindustrial society is not predictable, automatic, or even necessarily probable. All one can say is that there does appear to be a tendency toward this metamorphosis. The forces that could produce such a transformation were set in motion long ago and in one way or another will play themselves out. In the same sense that a seedling seeks sunlight or adolescents seek to establish their own identity (in ways that are often unconscious), so we may say that society shows signs of attempting a transformation—even though most of the participants are relatively oblivious to what impels them.

Nonetheless, there is no guarantee that this approaching transformation will proceed to completion. Various other outcomes are also possible. Our industrialized society could simply disintegrate. Just as the time came when the Romans could no longer keep their aqueducts repaired, so we might reach a time when we could not again assemble either the political will or the technical skill to orbit a man in space.

If a mutation of this magnitude is in progress why is it not more evident? Partly because the actor in such a historic drama suffers from myopia—he sees the events, but not the pattern they compose. Moreover, our collective anxiety about the future may cause us to unconsciously conspire *not* to see the significance of contemporary events.

Individuals and Societies in Transformation

Societies behave in some ways like individuals; their behavior in crisis exhibits some characteristics of individuals under stress. To be more

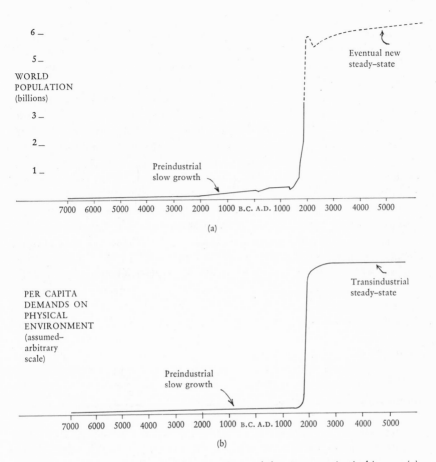

Figure 1. Two curves illustrating the uniqueness of the present point in history: (a) world population, and (b) per capita demands on the physical environment.

specific, study of the role that unconscious processes play in individual change suggests such unconscious processes may play a similar role in social change.

The phenomenon is well known in psychotherapy: The client will resist and avoid the very knowledge he most needs to resolve his problems. A similar situation exists for society as a whole. Both anthropology and history provide suggestive evidence that a society tends to hide knowledge from itself that is superficially threatening to the status quo, even though this knowledge may in fact be badly needed to resolve its most fundamental problems. This point cannot be overstressed. We are perplexed by contemporary societal problems not so much because of their essential complexity as because of unconscious resistance to clear perception of them.

The typical neurotic has a life-style that once worked reasonably well —that is why he adopted it. Conditions changed, however, and his old behavior patterns became inappropriate. The rational thing for him to do would be to assess the situation carefully, decide what new behavior patterns are called for, and change accordingly. But that is precisely what he does *not* do, because awareness of the need for fundamental change would be too threatening. Instead, he unconsciously attempts to hide his situation from himself and becomes more firmly locked into his old life-style. If his neurotic activity becomes sufficiently inappropriate in his current environment, he eventually may have a nervous breakdown. This breakdown may jar him loose from his old ways so forcibly that something different has to happen. With care and understanding he may undergo a fundamental reexamination of his life, and rebuild it on a new basis. If he is less fortunate, or if the environment is inadequately supportive, the breakdown may become permanent and he may never again be a fully functioning member of society.

Something parallel to the neurotic's mental breakdown may be occurring now in the technologically advanced world. There are numerous signs that we may be approaching a "societal nervous breakdown": tradeoffs between inflation and unemployment and between energy and environment grow increasingly intolerable; problems of world poverty seem ever farther from resolution; indications of fundamental alienation change form but fail to abate; and, above all, the erosion of past goals and values continues, coupled with a growing sense that no one knows where the society is heading—or should head. Yet the implication of these signs—that the old order is becoming unworkable —is extraordinarily threatening and largely resisted.

Alcoholics Anonymous has had a great deal of experience dealing with one type of individual transformation, that from drunkenness to sobriety. Much of the organization's experience is encapsulated in its "Twelve Steps." The first two are crucial, and the most difficult. They are:

1. We admitted we were powerless over alcohol—that our lives had become unmanageable.
2. We came to believe that a Power greater than ourselves could restore us to sanity.

Every alcoholic shrinks from accepting the first of these propositions, and the second is likely to remind him of the claims made by a religion he may have discarded long ago. Typically he flounders about until he hits rock bottom, when the unmanageability of his life becomes un-avoidably evident. At this point he may find creative potentialities be-yond his ego-self that make it possible for him to rebuild his life on a new and sounder base.

The industrialized world, intoxicated with the trappings of a ma-terially extravagant society, may be approaching its own rock-bottom phase. Something like the first two steps of A.A. may be needed, and society will resist them just as strongly as the alcoholic does. The first critical step is to admit that we face a set of dilemmas, of thwarted goals and intolerable trade-offs that make society unmanageable. The second step is to recognize that the image of man and his potentialities implicit in the premises of the industrial era is inadequate for meeting the challenge ahead, and that a new image of man could help restore society to health.

Just as the first two steps of A.A. cannot be proven (enabling the alcoholic to deny them to himself, even though his plight is obvious to others), neither can these two steps for societal transformation be proven or disproven. Realization may be postponed indefinitely, which will only make the ultimate transition that much more difficult.

Probably no one can say with certainty whether a transformation of industrial society has already begun—or whether it will ever occur. But if we remember that the future as well as the past can shape the course of present events, we see the potential importance of the transindustrial image, and of understanding the requirements of the transition. This knowledge could make the difference between a constructive and a disruptive outcome. A homely metaphor may help get this point across. If one understands the dynamics and develops sufficient skill, he can learn to ride a surfboard. However, if there is no wave, he cannot create one; if there is a wave, he cannot stop it. But if there is a wave and if he can ride a surfboard, then he is in a position very different from the one he would be in without that skill.

In much the same way, if we could understand the historical forces that appear to be bringing about a profound transformation of indus-trialized society, we would be better able to deal with them. If the forces are really not there, or are not strong enough, wishing and manipulating will not bring about a transformation. If the forces are there, a transfor-mation is probably beyond our power to stop. But if they are there and we understand them, we might be able to move with them in such a way that the transformation becomes an exhilarating ride instead of a crash-ing disaster.

The Magician by Rembrandt

CHAPTER ONE

THE METHODS OF FUTURES RESEARCH

AMONG THOSE WHO ARE future watchers, even those with impeccable credentials, there is considerable disagreement. Certainly not all scholars of the future find an imminent transformation of industrialized society in their crystal balls. For instance, Herman Kahn, director of the Hudson Institute and coauthor of *The Next 200 Years*, offers an impressive case for a "postindustrial perspective" in which, within the next century, "the more desperate and seemingly eternal problems of human poverty will have largely been solved or greatly alleviated" and "most misery will derive from the anxieties and ambiguities of wealth and luxury, not from physical suffering due to scarcities." Kahn believes that pollution, resource depletion, food and energy shortages, technological excesses, the gaping disparities between rich and poor nations, and the supposed deterioration of the quality of life are not insurmountable problems—if appropriate technological and institutional approaches are used to resolve them. He postulates that "the postindustrial economy should be close to a humanistic utopia by most historical standards"—if we do not falter or lose our nerve by succumbing to the "limits-to-growth" argument that economic growth must be precipitately slowed down because we are approaching planetary limitations. Kahn concludes, "New technology and capital investment are necessary . . . to help protect and improve the environment, to keep resource costs down, and to provide an economic surplus for problems and crises. . . . If we are reasonably prudent and flexible we will not have to contend with any really serious shortages in the medium run, and the long run looks even better." In other words, as Kahn sees it, there is no systemic crisis—just a crisis of will.

Other technological optimists, such as Daniel Bell, agree that there is no need for or likelihood of systemic transformation. In *The Coming of Post-Industrial Society* Bell predicts that there will be sufficient growth in service occupations and knowledge-based industries to provide work for all, and he expects that advancing technology will bring societal problems under control.

Many other futures researchers, however, see a need for, and signs of, some sort of systemic transformation. In *An Inquiry Into the Human Prospect* Robert Heilbroner presents a strong argument attesting to the need for such a transformation but doubts that we will achieve it. He explains, "The long-term solution requires nothing less than the gradual abandonment of the lethal techniques, the uncongenial ways of life, and the dangerous mentality of industrial civilization itself. . . . The [nearer-term] outlook is for convulsive change—change forced upon us by external events rather than by conscious choice, by catastrophe rather than by calculation. . . . If we ask whether it is possible to meet the challenges of the future without the payment of a fearful price, the answer must be: There is no such hope."

Some humanistic optimists writing about the future see the need for systemic transformation (away from the emphasis on materialistic values and economic growth and toward a more humane and person-centered society) and believe it can be brought about without causing a serious disruption of society. Charles Reich, author of *The Greening of America,* and George Leonard, author of *The Transformation*, are examples. This group pays little regard to the powerful institutionalized forces that would resist such profound systemic change. Thus, their romantic vision lacks an element of realism.

This diversity of forecasts raises the question as to whether we have any reliable basis for making forecasts of the future. In other words, is there anything to the esoteric art of futures research?

Six Principles Underlying Futures Research

Every action decision implies some assumption about the future; it is the function of futures research to make those assumptions explicit. Since we cannot know the future precisely, we must delineate alternative possibilities so that choices can be tested against various future states that *could* occur. But which futures are feasible and which are not? That is the central question of futures research.

If one presumes to say anything at all about the future of a social system, he must assume that there is something *dependable* about the behavior of that system. There are relatively few distinct ways in which social systems are dependable. The different methods of futures research are based essentially on various combinations of six principles that characterize complex, highly interconnected social systems.

One: Continuity. First of all, societies exhibit continuity. Social systems change smoothly from one state to another; generally they do not change in discontinuous jumps. (Even during relatively disruptive and seemingly discontinuous periods, such as the American Civil War or the French Revolution, much of the culture, social roles, and institutional framework of a society persists without fundamental change.) Thus, in making forecasts we commonly and reasonably extrapolate from past experience. This principle of continuity is used in all sorts of projections of trends and cycles—for forecasting demographic trends, economic cycles, and annual energy consumption; for anticipating future attitudes from polling data; for estimating future financial performance —to mention only a few.

Kahn and coauthor Anthony Wiener provide an interesting example of extrapolation from the past to forecast possible alternative futures in *The Year 2000: A Framework for Speculation.* They observe in the evolutionary development of Western society over many centuries a "basic long-term multifold trend." This trend consists of a number of basic tendencies—for example, Western culture has become increasingly manipulative, utilitarian, and based on rational thought and the senses rather than on intuition; technological change has become increasingly institutionalized; and industrialization and urbanization have expanded (see Table 1). Extrapolating from these long-term tendencies, they postulate alternative future possibilities that involve relatively minor or slow variations from this central multifold trend. (Kahn has subsequently altered his view and sees some indication of eventual modification of the multifold trend, but expects any major shift to take a century or more.)

In *The Coming of Post-Industrial Society* Daniel Bell provides a scholarly case of extrapolative social forecasting. He contends that the technologically advanced society of the future will increasingly depend upon theoretical knowledge as the prime source of innovation and of policy formulation. To arrive at the characteristics of postindustrial society, he projects this tendency, along with other components of the multifold trend, including two elements not specifically identified by Kahn. Bell writes:

The decisive social change taking place in our time — because of the interdependence of men and the aggregative character of economic actions, the rise of externalities and social costs, and the need to control the effects of technical change—is the subordination of the economic function of the political order. . . . The second major historical change is the sundering of social function [or place in society, primarily occupational] from property.

From this projection he derives his description of postindustrial society, distinguished by a high fraction of the working force in service and knowledge industries and by the commanding role of a technocratic elite.

It should be noted that the postindustrial society as described by Bell essentially involves a continuation of the long-term multifold trend. It seems reasonable enough that these central tendencies which have persisted for eight centuries or so would continue a while longer; yet, clearly these component trends are among the aspects of the old order that are currently being challenged. The social forecast of a transindustrial society postulates a future society that differs fundamentally from the postindustrial society discussed by both Bell and Kahn. Such a transformation to a transindustrial society presumes that a major departure from the long-term multifold trend will occur before the end of the present century.

Two: Self-consistency. A second guiding principle underlying futures research is that societal systems tend to be internally self-consistent. That is, the behavior of one sector of society does not generally contradict that of another. For instance, basic research is not likely to be well supported and flourishing when the economy is depressed.

The principle of self-consistency underlies one of the popular, if less systematic, techniques for examining the future—namely, scenario writing. The purpose of writing scenarios about the future is to insure that the characteristics asserted, whether arrived at from trend projections or other methods, "hang together" and make a reasonable story. A plausible future has to feel like it might be lived in. Familiar examples of scenario writing include Edward Bellamy's *Looking Backward*, Aldous Huxley's *Brave New World*, and George Orwell's *1984.*

Three: Similarities among social systems. Because the individuals making up varied social systems have fundamental characteristics in common, the systems themselves inevitably exhibit certain similarities. Accordingly, one group will tend to behave somewhat like another under similar circumstances. This observation of similarities across groups is used in anthropological approaches to the study of the future, in gaming methods where an individual assumes the role of a group or

Table 1: The Long-Term Multifold Trend of Western Culture

---

1. Increasingly sensate (empirical, this-worldly, secular, humanistic, pragmatic, manipulative, explicitly rational, utilitarian, contractual, epicurean, hedonistic, etc.) cultures.
2. Bourgeois, bureaucratic, and meritocratic elites.
3. Centralization and concentration of economic and political power.
4. Accumulation of scientific and technical knowledge.
5. Institutionalization of technological change, especially research, development, innovation, and diffusion.
6. Increasing military capability.
7. Westernization, modernization, and industrialization.
8. Increasing affluence and (recently) leisure.
9. Population growth.
10. Urbanization, recently suburbanization and "urban sprawl"—soon the growth of megalopoli.
11. Decreasing importance of primary and (recently) secondary occupations; increasing importance of tertiary and (recently) quaternary occupations.
12. Increasing literacy and education and (recently) the "knowledge industry" and increasing role of intellectuals.
13. Innovative and manipulative social engineering—i.e., rationality increasingly applied to social, political, cultural, and economic worlds as well as to shaping and exploiting the material world.
14. Increasing universality of the multifold trend.
15. Increasing tempo of change in all the above.

Additional components that seem more important than they did a few years ago:

16. Increasing scale of environmental impact of human activities.
17. Increasing rate of use of "nonrenewable" natural resources of minerals and fossil fuels.
18. Movement toward a single world economy with closely linked worldwide economic institutions.
19. Increasing gap between rich and poor populations.
20. Increasing subordination of the economic function to the political order (Bell).
21. Decreasing importance of private property (Bell).

Source: The Hudson Institute (Herman Kahn and Bruce Briggs, 1972).

a nation, and in cross-cultural comparisons (e.g., of stages of economic development).

Historical analogies in particular, if not carried too far, can be useful in suggesting possible future scenarios. For example, studies of historical occurrences of revolutionary cultural and political transformations suggest possible parallels today.

Four: Cause-effect relationships. Social systems exhibit apparent cause-effect connections or statistical correlations that imply cause and effect relationships. For instance, when making economic projections we assume that if scarcities occur, prices will rise; or that if the rate of inflation is lowered by manipulating the money supply, unemployment will increase. Such presumed cause-effect linkages underlie much economic and simulation modeling. They are the basis for the models in the Club of Rome's study *The Limits to Growth* which has generated much controversy since its publication in 1972. They form the basic principle in the widely used method of cross-impact analysis (in which aspects of the future are studied through the presumed interactions of contributing events on one another).

Five: Holistic trending. In their process of evolving and changing, social systems behave like integrated organic wholes. They have to be perceived in their entirety; thus there is no substitute for human observation and judgment about the future state of a system. To overcome the problem of bias of an individual observer, collective opinion can be sought in various ways. One of these is the so-called Delphi technique wherein the opinions of a number of judges are systematically processed and the results fed back to each of the judges as additional input, the object being to obtain refined judgments (but not necessarily consensus).

Six: Goal seeking. Societies have goals. They act with apparent intentionality, although the goals that might be inferred from observation are not necessarily declared ones. Just as individuals have aims of which they are but dimly aware, so do societies seek destinies that they have never explicitly proclaimed. In short, social change is not aimless, however obscured the goal. Modern industrialized society is confronted with a set of dilemmas that it seeks to resolve. Goals that once inspired commitment and loyalty no longer have the same power, and new priorities are being formed. The possible futures are distinguished, as much as anything, by the ways society seeks resolution of its dilemmas, and by the kinds of new goals that emerge.

Limitations of Futures Research

Various systematic approaches have been devised utilizing these six principles. Some approaches are strongly holistic while others concentrate on particular aspects of the society; some deal primarily with quantitative information (economic indicators, age distribution, population statistics, migration patterns, etc.) and other hard data about technological developments and ecological shifts, while others place more emphasis on factors that are hard to quantify, such as social innovations and shifts in cultural values and attitudes. Regardless of the approach, futures research inevitably remains more art than science, if only because of human unpredictability, perverseness, and creativity.

It is extremely difficult, whatever analysis or research method may be used, to achieve enough objectivity about the future to avoid being misled. We are not referring here to an idealized "value-free" position, which is sometimes mistakenly assumed to be characteristic of pure science. Rather, the aim is to achieve the kind of nonattachment and freedom from bias that a judge strives for in a court of law. Bias seems inevitable, especially with any single research approach. If the method deals primarily with numerical data, there is bias in favor of information that is easily quantifiable. If the method concentrates on theoretical issues and rational analysis, it may slight irrational and unconscious forces. The method may be biased by an implicit image of man—as free and rational or as unfree and controlled by his drives, habits, and social roles. It may be biased by a Malthusian pessimism or a technocratic optimism. Bias can be offset somewhat by deliberately employing several diverse approaches, synthesizing the results where they complement one another and carrying out further analyses when results conflict.

It is particularly difficult to overcome the bias that results from being immersed in a particular culture—from living in a particular area of the globe at a particular time in history. One is a product of his culture. Every culture has its blind spots, and there is no reason to suppose that ours is an exception. The anthropologist studying a primitive tribe, or the foreign traveler, sees things that the native misses; the historian is aware of characteristics of a particular period that were not apparent to the person living at that time. It is as difficult for a futures researcher to be objective today as it was for a scholar in the Middle Ages to comprehend what the post-Copernican world might be like.

Generating Alternative Futures—Simplified

We have identified six principles that can be used to test a described future (or trend) for plausibility. Still, much uncertainty about the future remains—because our knowledge of the present state of affairs and our comprehension of historical trends is imperfect, because unpredictable random events can affect the future, and because human choice is essentially unpredictable.

This uncertainty is to be recognized and honored. Consequently one cannot talk prudently about a single predicted future, but rather must describe several plausible futures. The six principles of futures research can be used, in a variety of ways, to delineate a set of alternative future paths that society might follow. The primary utility of generating alternative plausible futures is that contemplated action decisions can be tested against these different future contexts to determine under what conditions these projected decisions would appear to be appropriate and to alert the decision maker to future contexts in which these choices might be disastrous. Thus decision making becomes a dynamic pro-

The Opening of the Fifth and Sixth Seals by Albrecht Dürer

cess, in which the unfolding future prompts a continuing reexamination of available options and their probable consequences.

Here are two examples that illustrate how the basic principles of futures research may be applied in a systematic way. Carried out superficially these approaches could form the basis for an entertaining "futures game." Performed more earnestly and systematically they have been used effectively in serious research to generate plausible alternative futures.

Divergence mapping. For the first version describe 22 possible states of society that seem to be feasible in the United States within the next quarter century. Make particular use of the principles of continuity (the descriptions cannot be too different from a reasonable projection of past trends) and of internal self-consistency. Each description might consist of a characteristic title and a set of phrases describing salient features of the society. Remember, each one must feel as though it could be lived in. The following titles may serve to suggest what some of these states might involve:

Capitalism Reborn	Economic Drift
Edge of Holocaust	Hyperinflation
Recycling Society	Contented Maturity
Technological Success	House Divided
Bleak Prospect	Holding Pattern
Bouncy Prosperity	Welfare State
Moated America	The Inner Way
Road to Nationalization	Regimented Rationing
Dreary Stagnation	Global Cooperation
Communitarian Harmony	Chaotic Disruption

Now imagine each of these descriptions as a frame in a motion picture of the future. Put them together in plausible sequences. First go through the 22 descriptions and identify the four frames most like the present. Insofar as this seems possible, order these in some natural way (e.g., least to most successful, politically closed to open, centralized to decentralized) and consider them as frames *a* through *d* in the 22-frame array of *Figure 2.* Next identify the seven frames least like the present, order them roughly in the same way, and consider them as frames *p* through *v* in the diagram. Complete the divergence map by filling in the intermediate frames with the remaining descriptions. It may take a little adjusting and even the substitution of new descriptions until you get a map that satisfies you.

You now have a simple map of alternative paths to the future—perhaps more accurately, alternative stepping stones. For example,

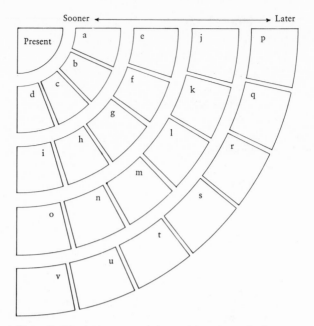

Figure 2. Divergence map of alternative paths to the future.

one route to the future might pass through frames *c-g-l-s*. Another might diverge from this and go through frames *c-g-m-t*. These paths need to be examined for plausibility using the six basic principles.

Finally, go through the most plausible paths and assign some sort of time scale to each. By what year might each given state be reached? When you complete this exercise you will have thought a great deal— perhaps more systematically and holistically than you ever have before —about future conditions that might actually occur.

A more elaborate method. Let us look briefly at a second approach, one that is capable of expansion into a full-fledged systematic futures research technique. Consider a number of sectors of the society, such as:

    E Economic performance
    S Economic structure
    T Science and technology
    C Cultural transmission and change
    A Personal aims and concerns
    P Political structure

For each of these, define about a half-dozen alternative states that together span the reasonable range of possibilities—for example:

E_1 Widespread prosperity
E_2 Prosperity restricted to certain socioeconomic groups
E_3 Equilibrium, slow economic growth; general public satisfaction
E_4 Recession, slow economic growth; general public dissatisfaction
E_5 Economic depression

Thus, the state of society could be abbreviated into a code word such as $E_2S_1T_3C_5A_5P_1$. The total number of possible states that can be so described is very large, of course, but the vast majority would not be plausible. For example, using the principle of internal self-consistency, we can argue that if T_2 represented well-supported and aggressive scientific and technological development, the condition T_2 is not likely to exist when the nation is in the grip of an economic depression. Thus the combination E_5T_2 would be ruled out, and all the states containing that combination would be removed from further consideration. Furthermore, employing the principle of continuity, it becomes clear that only relatively continuous sequences of states are plausible, thus eliminating still more possibilities. Utilizing arguments like these, a relatively small number of code-word sequences remain as plausible paths to the future. Such analyses have indeed been carried out and prove to be useful in identifying alternative plausible futures.

In the next chapter we will examine several of these alternative futures more carefully. Up to now we have been dealing with abstract possibilities. But the futures to be considered next should be of particular interest because we will have to live through one of them, like it or not.

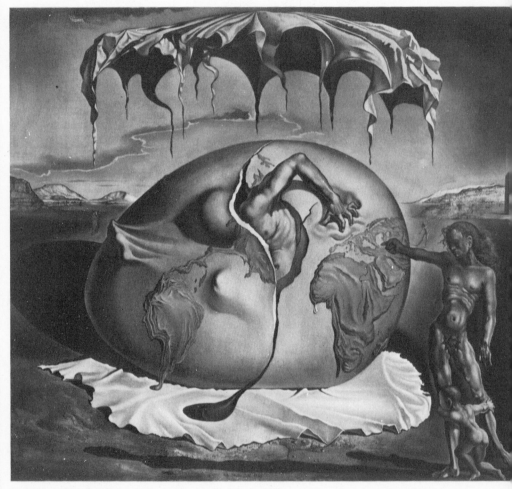

Geopoliticus Child Watching the Birth of a New Man by Salvador Dali

CHAPTER TWO

A TRANSFORMATION AHEAD?

LEWIS MUMFORD OBSERVED in *The Transformations of Man* that there have probably been no more than a half-dozen profound transformations of Western society since the time of primitive man. Each of these, Mumford states, "rested on a new metaphysical and ideological base; or rather, upon deeper stirrings and intuitions whose rationalized expression takes the form of a new picture of the cosmos and the nature of man." Thus, during the founding of the great world religions, at the fall of the Roman Empire, or at the end of the Middle Ages there were not only major changes in social roles and institutions, but more fundamentally in cultural premises, in dominant values—and in man's very image of himself.

What are the implications of suggesting that industrialized society may be on the verge of such a fundamental transformation, perhaps more wrenching than any that preceded it because of the rapidity at which we are approaching it, more extensive because it involves all parts of the globe, and more thoroughgoing because of the depth at which the cultural premises are shaken?

Varieties of Societal Problems

The problems of society can be viewed from various levels. We are all aware that this nation and the world are beset by numerous societal problems: poverty, crime, racism, pollution, unemployment, inflation, drug abuse, social disruptions, famine, the threat of nuclear war, and the like. We are equally aware that direct measures for dealing with these problems have, on the whole, been unsuccessful and have often led to unanticipated and undesired consequences. Thus, price and wage controls offer temporary relief from inflation, but in the end tend to leave us in a worse position than before. Urban renewal programs designed to improve housing conditions for the poor often leave them with their old neighborhoods destroyed and unable to afford available alternatives. Welfare regulations instituted to improve the lot of ghetto children have contributed to family breakdown by making it economically advantageous for mothers to raise their children in a fatherless home. Minimum wage laws intended to aid unskilled workers have actually made it more difficult for many to find employment; at the higher rates of pay, employers find it more economical to replace people with machines or to eliminate jobs. Legislation and programs dedicated to the reduction of inequalities of opportunity between the races (such as the busing of schoolchildren) have instead heightened interracial tensions.

The reasons for these failures may be intrinsic. These problems appear to be symptoms of underlying conditions that are more fundamental and more difficult to delineate. When the treatment has concentrated on removing one symptom, it has often exacerbated another. It is, accordingly, no accident that planned social measures have produced results which were just the opposite of those intended by their well-meaning sponsors.

All of these observations suggest that there is a second level at which the ills of society may be viewed. Accordingly, some analysts, including the radical group, have argued that the 1960s-type liberal programs for problem eradication are intrinsically flawed—that the miseries of the poor, the injustices experienced by minorities, the violences committed by the socially disaffected, the squandering of natural resources, the ravaging of the environment can be alleviated only through basic structural reform in society itself. They maintain that society's problems lie at the level of basic institutions, built-in distributions of economic and political power, and social roles that people have been taught to assume. They hold that fundamental remedies are required—altering institutions to incorporate less economic and political injustice and to produce less intolerance, hypocrisy, racism, and greed; creating incentive and regulatory structures to reduce exploitation of people and environment; and restructuring social programs so that they do not depend upon persuading people to act against their own perceived self-interest.

Another group of analysts sees the ultimate resolution of the problem in a still more fundamental transformation of society. They have argued that there is a third level at which to view society's problems, underlying and more basic than the level of institutions and social roles. This third level involves the most basic assumptions, attitudes, and values held by individuals and institutionalized in the culture. When this part of the social structure no longer accords with reality—leading the society toward conditions that are intolerable by its own standards—a fundamental crisis looms. In such a case, difficult and thoroughgoing transmutation seems to be the only way in which the complex, interwoven maze of societal problems could achieve satisfactory resolution.

To urge that these third-level problems of deep cultural incongruities press for attention is not to argue that problems at the other two levels should be ignored. One sometimes encounters a kind of simplistic faith that the problems of the world would solve themselves if only everyone would experience the right religious or moral or ideological transformation. But the physician who diagnoses a patient's disease as psychosomatic in origin does not withold symptomatic relief because he perceives the patient's attitude toward life to be the underlying problem. Likewise, it is neither reasonable nor politically conceivable that current ameliorative measures should be halted because a more fundamental explanation for societal ills has been uncovered. On the contrary, the experience of trying solutions that fail, and the acts of challenging institutions and confronting habitual behaviors are among the important ways of fostering changes in basic belief and value patterns.

As we proceed to examine the forces for social transformation, the primary focus will be on the United States—on the U.S. as part of the world system, to be sure, but we will be describing problems in the particular form they assume in this country. For Sweden, Japan, and other highly industrialized capitalist countries the description would be somewhat different. For Russia or East Germany it would be more different still. From the viewpoint of the nations of the Third World, some of the same problems would appear, but as if from the opposite end of the telescope. If any large-scale change occurs all nations will be affected. It is not unduly parochial, however, to concentrate on the form that change might take in our own particular part of the system.

There will be little discussion herein of the threat of nuclear war. Attempts at resolving this problem will and must be pursued by statesmen around the globe. But nuclear conflict will remain an ever-present danger as long as the fundamental dilemmas remain, the world inequities continue or worsen, and a partial breakdown of the world system is a serious possibility. Both diplomatic and technological approaches to removing the nuclear threat are probably futile if the underlying (third-level) problems remain. It is as if a marriage counselor is dealing with a warring man and wife, each of whom sleeps with a loaded pistol under the pillow. There is little gained by trying to convince them they should sleep with butcher knives instead.

The Industrial-Era Paradigm

In further exploring the meaning of a fundamental societal transformation it will be useful to introduce the term "dominant paradigm." Originally simply synonymous with pattern or model, paradigm has come to have a more specific meaning since its use by T.S. Kuhn in his seminal study *The Structure of Scientific Revolutions* (1962). Thus we shall use the term dominant paradigm to refer to *the basic way of perceiving, thinking, valuing, and doing, associated with a particular vision of reality.*

A dominant paradigm is seldom if ever stated explicitly; it exists as unquestioned, tacit understanding that is transmitted through the culture and to succeeding generations through direct experience (rather than being "taught"). A paradigm cannot be defined precisely in a few well-chosen sentences. In fact, it is not something to be expressed verbally at all. It is what the anthropologist hopes to understand after he has lived in a foreign culture for a long time—what the natives in a society perceive with their eyes and value with their feelings. A dominant paradigm encompasses more than an ideology or a world view but less than a total culture.

In retrospect we can see that our present Western, industrial-era paradigm began its climb to dominance several centuries ago. It has since had a major impact upon all aspects of Western society and Japan, and has had a significant influence on the rest of the world. This paradigm differs sharply from the dominant paradigm of the Middle Ages in Europe. Among the characteristic features of the industrial-era paradigm are the following:

1. *Industrialization* of the production of goods and services is a predominant theme, achieved by organizing and subdividing work into increasingly elemental (and less intrinsically significant) increments, and replacing human labor by machines. Industrialization leads toward goals of labor productivity and a higher material standard of living.

2. The *scientific method* is the supreme mode of inquiry. Science is wedded to technology such that the scientific search for knowledge is predominantly utilitarian, with prediction and control as its guiding values, and technological progress as its goal.

3. The paradigm implies belief in unlimited *material progress*, in man's expanding control over nature, and in his unlimited ability to

understand the universe from the data provided by his physical senses. Acquisitive materialism is a central operative value.

4. *Pragmatic values* predominate, with the individual free to seek his own self-interest, as he defines it, in the marketplace. Hence the future is not determined by tradition nor achieved through organized plan, but rather it happens as a consequence of relatively autonomous units in the system pursuing their own practical ends.

In *The Transformations of Man* Mumford vividly summarizes the vast change that was involved in shifting from the old feudal paradigm of the Middle Ages to the new, industrial-era paradigm: "Within the span of a few centuries the focus of interest shifted from the inner world to the outer world. . . . All but one of the [seven deadly] sins, sloth, was transformed into a positive virtue. Greed, avarice, envy, gluttony, luxury, and pride were the driving forces of the new economy. . . . Unbounded power was harnessed to equally unbounded appetites."

Paradigm Lost?

Born out of this industrial-era paradigm have been the fabulous products of modern industrial organization and technology. Yet this paradigm is clearly showing signs of a breakdown, for its greatest successes are presently leading to major societal problems. The remarkable success of modern public health measures in reducing infant mortality and death rates from disease has led to problems of overpopulation. Achievements in lengthening the adult life span have brought problems in care of the aged. Advances in nuclear and biological weaponry have brought, not security from enemies, but the threat of mass destruction. Technological developments in communication and transportation have given us the political volatility of a shrinking world as well as increased air and noise pollution. Success at generating widespread affluence has aggravated environmental spoliation and resource depletion. Automated production systems have created monotonous and dehumanizing jobs and, with further automation, unemployment. The list is nearly endless.

These "problems of technological success" worsen steadily. The trade-offs (e.g., economic growth *vs.* environmental quality) grow more and more intolerable. Their origins are inherent in the characteristics of the industrial-era paradigm and thus the problems may be ultimately unresolvable without a major shift away from that paradigm.

This threatened breakdown of the industrial-era paradigm can be summarized as comprising five fundamental failures:

1. *It fails to promote one of the most fundamental functions of a society, namely, to provide each individual with an opportunity to con-*

tribute to the society and to be affirmed by it in return. This failure involves much more than an inability to achieve reasonably full employment. The basic problem is that the structure of society has the effect of defining an ever-increasing number of people as "unneeded." They are, in fact, not needed for production, and with the industrial mind-set this becomes equated with being extraneous and useless. The lurking shortage of work roles has provoked anxiety for the past half century, though this problem has been diminished by the economic stimulus of wars and preparations for war.

In his book *Cybernation: The Silent Conquest* (1962) Donald Michael forecast that the shortage of work roles would be a key problem in the future. For a few years it seemed that his warning might have been a cry of wolf and that new technology would generate more jobs than it displaced. But the new constraints of environmental degradation and resource scarcities changed that. Production cannot increase indefinitely; superfluous persons cannot be provided jobs through ever-expanding production. As Margaret Mead succinctly put it: "The unadorned truth is that we do not need now, and will not need later, much of the marginal labor—the very young, the very old, the very uneducated, and the very stupid." Ironically, although technology can potentially relieve men of burdensome and routine labor, it has in fact deprived many men and women of the privilege of performing wholesome, mind-forming, self-rewarding, appreciated work.

2. *It fails to foster more equitable distribution of power and justice.* A fundamental power instability is intrinsic to any conceivable society: Those who possess knowledge or physical, political, or economic power in any society are in the best position to gain more, while those who lack knowledge or power are less likely to acquire it. In the vernacular, "Them as has, gets." Because this power instability can ultimately destroy the social fabric, every stable society has had to devise some way of counteracting it, including some form of legitimized coercion. (This has been accomplished in many ways: Traditional societies often have caste structures, wherein certain rights are granted each caste level; some small societies have egalitarian communist structures and ethics. In every case some limiting mechanism ultimately counteracts the tendency of power to accumulate indefinitely.)

In a modern industrial democracy the tendency for power to accumulate is held in check by traditions of equality of opportunity and of socioeconomic mobility, reinforced by a variety of regulating measures—antitrust laws, fair trade agreements, graduated income tax, checks and balances in government, collective bargaining arrangements, regulatory commissions, and so forth. But these mechanisms have proven inadequate to bring about a more equitable distribution. This failure is partly due to the growth of giant corporations with such enormous economic power that they are relatively immune to normal processes of community control. More fundamentally, however, the mechanisms are unsuccessful because the basic paradigm itself contains no rationale for redistribution. That rationale has always been provided by an altruistic Judeo-Christian ethic based in transcendental values which were *external* to the basic paradigm of the industrial era—remnants of an earlier dominant paradigm. That ethic was seriously eroded during the 20th century by the rise of positivistic science and a materialistic world view. With the decline of what amounted to an American "civil religion" came a reduced efficacy of those social-regulation mechanisms that required it to function smoothly.

Even more seriously, perhaps, the industrial-era paradigm contains no rationale or incentive for more equitable distribution of the earth's resources between the industrialized nations and the Third World countries. The seeds of worldwide conflict lie in the enormous and growing disparity between the world's rich and poor peoples. On no grounds is the industrial paradigm more bitterly challenged.

3. *It fails to foster socially responsible management of the development and application of technology.* Many societal problems are the direct result of the unspoken "technological imperative" that whenever technology could make a profit for an individual or a corporation, or could contribute to a nation's ability to carry on warfare, it would be developed and applied. The result is that negative effects of technology —the polluted rivers, endangered species, hazards to public safety, undesirable social impacts, proliferating arms races—build up to intolerable levels before there is a serious attempt at corrective action. Some earlier control over the consequences of scientific and technological innovation is essential, both at the international and national level. If controls are to work, however, they will need to be supported by an ethic that values the general good more than private profit.

Both the failure to foster socially responsible technology management and the failure to achieve more equitable distribution of wealth grow directly out of a central weakness in the free-market system—its inability to place public needs above private gain. Socialist industrial states can apparently distribute wealth and regulate technological impact more successfully than states that are more dependent upon a free-market system, but socialist states pay for their gains by having to rely more heavily on central control, with its attendant risks of bureaucratic stultification and authoritarian inflexibility.

4. *It fails to provide goals that will enlist the deepest loyalties and*

commitments of the nation's citizens. Material economic growth and affluence are not enough. Although the industrial-era paradigm has contributed to the solution of most of the how-to-do-it questions we can imagine, it fails to shed light on the question of *what is worth doing.* Again it is important to note that those goals which have in the past enlisted the nation's deepest loyalties and commitments are part of the Western political tradition based on Judeo-Christian principles whose force has declined as the industrial-era paradigm gained in dominance. For example, the Declaration of Independence asserts, "We hold these truths to be self-evident, that all men are created equal, that they are endowed by their Creator with certain inalienable Rights . . ." and to the deductions from those truths concludes, "we mutually pledge . : . our Lives, our Fortunes, and our Sacred Honor." Behavioral science had pronounced, by early in this century, that such action was either conditioned or neurotic behavior.

5. *It fails to develop and maintain the habitability of the planet.* The ethic that man can control and should exploit nature leads ineluctably to greater and greater disruption of previous ecological balances, ravaging of the environment, and squandering of natural resources.

These five failures are *intrinsic.* Various factors—population pressures, political developments, economic trends, etc.—might alter the timetable, but the failures are implicit in the paradigm itself and are awaiting only the unfolding of its consequences to become critical.

Paradigm Regained

The breakdown of the industrial-era paradigm and its replacement by another would be accompanied by drastic change in the society's operative values and institutions. More profoundly, it would involve a change in the basic perception of reality. We recall our definition of the social paradigm as "the basic way of perceiving, thinking, valuing, and doing, associated with a particular vision of reality." It is change in that vision of reality that is the hallmark of the historically rare fundamental transformation.

There are already signs of the emergence of a new paradigm. It will be useful to identify some of the essential characteristics now, although in doing so we anticipate arguments of later chapters. Key features of the emergent paradigm can be deduced from assuming that the new transindustrial paradigm will grow smoothly out of and will be rooted in the past, and that it will provide a setting in which the dilemmas of advanced industrialization become resolvable.

Some clues to the nature of the new paradigm come from survey and poll data that indicate significant shifts in the values and beliefs of

Americans in the last decade. Poll data by Daniel Yankelovich, for instance, show for both college student and corporate executive groups, starting in the late 1960s, distinct value shifts reflecting increased concern with humanistic and spiritual values, quality of life, and community; and diminishing emphasis on materialistic values and status goals. He called the emerging values a "New Naturalism." Similar shifts were observed for blue-collar workers a few years later.

A wide range of cultural indicators support this observation of a fundamental shift in values. They include the kinds of books people buy and read; the kinds of groups they join, their choice of self-development activities, and their use of leisure time; themes of plays and motion pictures; the frequency of topics appearing in magazine articles; and the appearance of a "New Age" subculture concerned with frugal and naturalistic lifestyles, esoteric knowledge, and the building of a more humanistic society. All of these indicators show swelling interest in two separate but related areas of concern. One is a reemergence of the age-old spiritual quest for inner awareness and a deeper understanding of man's relationship to the universe about him. The other involves social issues and environmental concerns and a growing questioning of the workability of the social system in its present form. Both of these themes loomed large in the student activities of the now legendary 1960s, although they were by no means restricted to the campuses.

The psychedelic-hippie and the human-potential movements gained prominence on college campuses in the early 1960s. However, the 1961 opening of the first so-called growth center, Esalen Institute at Big Sur, California, and the founding of the Association for Humanistic Psychology in the same year (both involving mainly persons well past college-student age) make it clear this was a broader cultural movement not restricted to the college-age youth. It was also very clear by the early 1970s that there was widespread and growing interest in mystical experience and meditative states; in consciousness-expanding activities ranging from yoga and transcendental meditation to psychedelic drugs and biofeedback; in the esoteric and arcane; and in research into a broad range of psychic phenomena. A "New Transcendentalism" was present in the culture—a visionary idealism emphasizing that man is more than the sum of his mundane experiences, he is a spiritual entity, and that ultimate reality is to be found in the realm of the spiritual and mystical rather than the material and empirical.

The other separate but related theme—that of political activism and the challenging of the system—came into visibility with the civil rights movement, which enlisted idealistic youths in increasing numbers for the dozen or so years following the U.S. Supreme Court decision in 1954

Ut Omnia Exsolvantur by Hans Erni

Courtesy Hans Erni, Lucerne

on racial segregation in the public schools (*Brown* v. *Board of Education*). By about 1964 the social and political issues broadened to include the university's entanglement with the military-industrial complex, the Vietnam war, and the draft. As the activist movement expanded still further into the larger society, it came to include issues of the environment, consumer and minority rights, Third World self-determination, and limits to growth.

The various components of these two streams of activity have interacted with one another, but at the same time they have remained distinct and diffuse so that there is nothing like a massive, organized, and unified political movement. Despite some relationship between these activities and traditional left-wing political movements, what we are witnessing is not a political revolutionary development. As some activists phrased it late in the 1960s, "The real revolution is in people's heads." This statement explains why the use of perception-changing techniques has played such a central role. These techniques are of two types. One type is mainly self-chosen and aimed at spiritual or transcendental awareness; it includes meditation, yoga, self-awareness exercises, various group and individual psychotherapies, and psychedelic drugs. The other type is largely imposed on others and is aimed at social and political awareness, that is, at perceiving aspects of the breakdown of the industrial-era paradigm and of oppressive elements of social institutions; examples are consumer and environmentalist confrontations, black-white and student-police confrontations, and political theater. These radicalizing techniques are similar in that they jolt the person out of his habitual perceptions so that he sees—as he has not before—both his own transcendental nature and the influences of social institutions.

Taken together, these challenges to diverse aspects of the industrial-era paradigm and its institutions support the view that a societal metamorphosis could be imminent. If it is, at the core of this transmutation would be a change in our most basic views about the meaning of human experience. Furthermore, if it is successful, we can anticipate that this transindustrial paradigm would include the following characteristics:

1. It would perceive that the fundamental *dilemmas of industrialized society* are rooted in the inadequacy of the value postulates of the industrial-era paradigm.

2. It would recognize that *science* has been shaped by the prediction-and-control values of the industrial-era paradigm, and that a science aimed at guiding the evolutionary development of man and society will place more emphasis on understanding and less on generating manipulative technology; it would view "explanations" (both scientific and religious) as useful metaphors and hence would see no necessary contra-

diction between scientific metaphors adapted to the objective physical world and the religious or metaphysical metaphors used in communicating about suprasensory experience.

3. It would assume the existence of a *spiritual order*, discoverable and explorable, and in some sense testable, against which human value choices could be assessed; emerging from this spirituality would be a creative work ethic, placing a high value on aware participation in both individual and social evolution. The primary emphasis would be on "to be," rather than "to have" or "to control."

4. It would embody an *ecological ethic* of concern for the whole, deriving from the transcendental order and unitary perception of reality.

5. It would involve a *teleological view* of life and evolution (as having direction and purpose); hence the future would be perceived to be partly shaped by human choices, guided by supraconscious evolutionary tendencies toward development of man's spiritual potentialities beyond the realm of his mundane experiences. Such a transindustrial paradigm would *extend* rather than *contradict* the contemporary scientific world view, much as relativity theory extended Newtonian mechanics. Moreover, its most fundamental postulates are not essentially new. They have comprised a central stream of thought in the humanities, in Western political tradition, and in transcendentalist movements in our own nation's history. They have, however, never formed the guiding paradigm of an entire society. Popular religions, both Eastern and Western, have included ethics similar to those implied by the five aforementioned characteristics. However, these traditional ethics have typically existed in an authoritarian context, rather than as discoverable and testable propositions of an open inquiry.

Transformation Anyone?

If such a paradigm, involving a basic shift in the accepted vision of reality, were to become the basis of presently industrialized society, its institutionalization would amount to one of the most thoroughgoing transformations in the history of mankind. We might apply to such a change the Greek word *metanoia*: "a fundamental transformation of mind," as in religious conversion. This transformation is to be distinguished from other changes that are revolutionary in a social or political sense but do not involve a significant change in the basic, implicit, unchallenged, taken-as-given metaphysic of the society.

Some futurists have noted that the 1970s appear to be a time of profound change, and have likened contemporary discontinuities to one or another great transformation in the past. Comparison is made with the Industrial Revolution, which involved profound institutional changes, with accompanying value and life-style changes. As in present times, the period was characterized by apparent advance on some fronts (e.g., manufacturing technology) and temporary regression on others (e.g., quality of life in the factory cities). Changes brought about by the Industrial Revolution encountered bitter opposition and strong resistance.

Somewhat similarly, in the case of the Copernican (or scientific) revolution there were profound changes in the basic concept of the nature of knowledge, in culturally held beliefs and values, and in social institutions. Scientific laws replaced theological explanations, values became more this-worldly, and beliefs shifted from supernatural to natural explanations. Science displaced the church as the official truth-seeking system. Again, changes brought about by the Copernican revolution were strongly resisted; there was a traumatic transition period with decades of religious wars.

And yet the changes of the Industrial and Copernican revolutions, profound as they were, amounted to no more than periods of accelerated working-out of aspects of the "basic long-term multifold trend" of Western society (defined in the previous chapter)—becoming over at least eight centuries increasingly more secular, this-worldly, utilitarian, empirical, sensate, manipulative, scientific, innovative, industrialized, urbanized, literate, and affluent. *We may now be entering a transformation that involves a basic alteration of that trend.* If so, we probably cannot postpone its appearance. We might possibly be able to affect its outcome. We almost surely *can* affect the amount of social disruption accompanying the change.

We need a way of thinking about the alternative possible futures we may confront; some graphics may help us. Imagine two dimensions along which we could plot the state of society at a given time. For example, let one be some measure of the society's ability to deal with the problems it faces—this might range from "inept and lacking vigor" to "able and energetic." A second dimension might be some measure of the degree of openness, mutual trust, and individual liberty allowed. Thus, the history of the society could be described graphically by plotting these two measures as they have changed through time. Similarly, the "future history," if we could know it, could be described by plotting the measures as they change through future time. But because of uncertainty about the future we must think in terms of alternative future histories.

An attempt to indicate this concept is shown in *Figure 3*. One possibility is that the arguments we will be following in this book are wrong —that there is no transformation under way. Hence, the industrial-era paradigm will remain dominant; past trends will continue into the future. Industrialization, technological advance, and economic growth

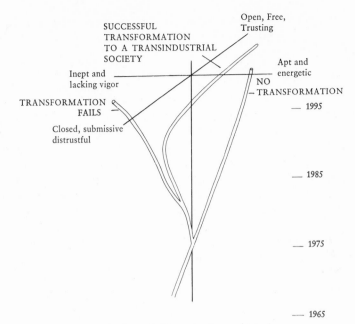

SUCCESSFUL
TRANSFORMATION
TO A TRANSINDUSTRIAL
SOCIETY

Open, Free,
Trusting

Inept and
lacking vigor

Apt and
energetic

NO
TRANSFORMATION

TRANSFORMATION
FAILS

— 1995

Closed, submissive
distrustful

— 1985

— 1975

— 1965

Figure 3. Several alternative future histories.

will accelerate as in the past; emphasis on productivity and efficiency will remain. Reliance on technological manipulations of social, political, cultural, and economic affairs will continue, as will exploitation of the material world.

A second "future history" would feature the transformation outlined here and discussed in more detail in Chapter Eight. If this future is to be reached through a nondisruptive transition to a transindustrial society, it must build on the past. Probably this means that most existing institutions (e.g., multinational corporations, the Congress, the stock market, the advertising industry, the military establishment) will remain with more or less the same external form, although their operative goals may be significantly or even drastically different from past goals.

A third future would assume that the forces for transformation are present, but that the disruptive stress is too much for society. Thus society will approach the end of the century with reduced technological capabilities and a general breakdown and disintegration of the system.

The main point is that the future is neither entirely predetermined nor completely open to choice. Some trajectories appear possible or plausible—perhaps even probable. Other trajectories do not even seem conceivable. Focusing on these three alternative possible futures suggests how to watch unfolding events of the next few years and draws attention to the factors that will make the difference between a successful and an unsuccessful transformation.

The Future Prospect

The prospect of living through a thoroughgoing societal transformation is sobering. History gives us scant cause for anticipating that we could escape without economic decline, political and social disruptions, and more extensive human suffering than most parts of the United States have ever experienced (the possible exception being portions of the South after the Civil War). A period of chaos seems inevitable as the powerful momentum of the industrial era is turned in a new direction and the various members and institutions of the society respond at different speeds.

Accurate interpretation of this disorder is crucial. The form—and success—of society's policies and actions will depend a great deal on whether the disruptions are seen as necessary steps in the change toward a more workable system or are perceived as capricious and essentially destructive.

At the same time we must recognize that we are talking about an

Gymnasion by Hans Erni

event that is historically improbable because of its rarity. It is a transformation that has not yet occurred; therefore there must be tentativeness in asserting that it is beginning and uncertainty in attempting to delineate its characteristics. Nonetheless, if this transindustrial transformation thesis turns out to be correct, the consequences for decision making in all portions of the society are profound. Hence we can ill afford to ignore the possibility.

The Reformation period lasted about a century. Earlier major transformations, such as the agricultural revolution, lasted far longer and were more widespread geographically. How could a shift as fundamental as the one we are postulating take place within a decade or two? One reason for thinking it plausible is the general acceleration of change. Another is the impact of modern communications media. Still another reason may lie, as we shall see, in the potentially broad acceptability of the replacement paradigm—both in industrialized countries and in the Third World—because of its compatibility with traditional belief systems around the world.

And so let us proceed to examine in more detail the outline sketched here. We will explore four fundamental dilemmas of the technologically and industrially advanced world to learn why they appear unresolvable in a society in which the industrial-era paradigm is dominant. These dilemmas are all contemporary forms of one or another of the classical economic problems of *employment, distribution,* and *regulation.* The crisis arises, ironically, because the industrial age has been so phenomenally successful in dealing with a fourth classical economic problem, that of *production.* After reviewing the four dilemmas we will examine salient aspects of a basic change in our very image of man himself—a change that points toward the central characteristics of the new paradigm. Finally we will attempt to outline some probable characteristics of the transindustrial society.

"*Excuse me, sir. I am prepared to make you a rather attractive offer for your square.*"

CHAPTER THREE

THE GROWTH DILEMMA

THE GROWTH DILEMMA besets not only this nation but the whole industrialized world—capitalist and socialist alike. The dilemma, simply stated, is that we cannot sustain the unregulated growth of the sort we have had in the past—but we cannot afford *not* to keep growing because of the massive economic consequences that would result from a halt to industrial growth. Stated more bluntly, the industrialized countries of the world are structured in such a way that their economies demand growth that the world's finite resources can support only with increasing difficulty.

The costs of material, economic, and technological growth are becoming increasingly intolerable; to understand why, we need only consider the present scarcities of:

- Fossil fuels and other sources of energy.
- Mineral and nonmineral resources.
- Fresh water.
- Arable land and habitable space.
- Waste-absorbing capacity of the natural environment.
- Resilience of the planet's life-supporting ecosystems.

We are simultaneously approaching the planetary limits for all of these resources; they must be considered together because they are interdependent. The problem is not that a critical shortage in any particular category is imminent; even if it were, substitutability provides a way out. One energy source can be exchanged for another; materials can be substituted for one another. Low-grade ores can be exploited, although this requires greater expenditures of energy and causes more severe consequences for the environment. Materials can be recycled, but that too takes energy, for collection as well as processing. More land can be turned to food production and present agricultural productivity increased, but this requires water and would consume more petroleum products for tractor fuel and fertilizer. The resulting pollution from runoffs of fertilizer and pesticides can be cleaned up with processes that require still more materials and energy. The difficulty is that, because *all* of these interdependent factors are approaching planetary limits together, the solutions that resolved scarcity problems in the past—geographic expansion and technological advancement—do not promise the same sort of relief in the future. Accordingly, the costs, to the economy and the environment, of continuing growth become greater and greater.

Slowing or stopping growth generates problems of a different sort. The most obvious and anxiety-producing cost is economic depression and unemployment. (We leave for the moment the question of whether economic dislocation irrevocably accompanies lowered growth; it is clear, however, that no one presently knows how to achieve a no-growth economy without crushing problems of unemployment.) A second important problem is the effect upon those at the low end of the economic scale. It is easier to redistribute a rapidly growing national income than one that is growing slowly. When the national income is growing rapidly, nearly everyone can be made better off in some material way; when growth slows down, the inequities become more conspicuous and incendiary. In terms of the familiar metaphor, as long as the economic pie is growing larger, the poor may be satisfied with their expanding piece, but they will no longer be satisfied if the pie ceases to enlarge.

Consequences of Growth

The concept of economic growth is relatively modern. Prior to the Industrial Revolution there was no general expectation that a country would grow steadily richer. By the middle of the 20th century, however, economic progress had become a standard hope and expectation. This new concern for growth had numerous political causes. Not only did growth provide steady improvement in the material standard of living, it also allowed people to evade the distasteful problem of finding mechanisms for effectively redistributing wealth. Moreover, a strong economic base contributed to national power and prestige, and rapid economic growth enabled governments to spend more on public services. It has also been argued, though perhaps less convincingly, that capitalism requires economic growth to survive, and that present environmental problems can only be solved with a strong economy.

The post-World War II era was one of unparalleled growth throughout the industrialized world. The characteristics of this growth are important to note. Surprisingly, the quantity of basic goods produced per capita did not increase appreciably during this period. What did change were the kinds of goods produced and the nature of productive technologies.

The technological transformation of the American farm is one of the developments that had the greatest social and environmental impact. Before it was transformed by modern technology, a farm was simply a place where certain biological activities were localized. Crops took nutrients from the soil; the nutrients came from organic matter; the soil's organic store was maintained by the return of plant debris and animal wastes to the soil and by the natural fixation of nitrogen from the air into a useful organic form. The ecological cycles tended to be in balance, and with care the natural fertility of the soil could be maintained indefinitely. In contrast, modern agribusiness is so intensive that it depletes the natural supply of organic nutrients; as a result, inorganic fertilizers are applied in increasing amounts, and their runoff from the fields pollutes water supplies. Wastes from cattle confined to feedlots accumulate and result in more water pollution; in the U.S., cattle produce more organic waste than the total sewage from humans. Furthermore, wide use of pesticides and genetically controlled plant varieties drastically alter the natural ecology. Finally, when the whole food production cycle is considered—from soil preparation, planting, cultivating, and harvesting, through transportation, processing, packaging, distribution, and final preparation—far more fossil fuel energy than solar energy from photosynthesis goes into the food on our table. Thus the trend toward further industrialization of agriculture may be less rational than has been assumed.

Another characteristic of postwar technology has been the progressive substitution of relatively nonbiodegradable synthetics for natural materials, and energy-costly materials and operations for less energy-intensive ones. Examples of the former are the substitution of nylon and polyester fibers for cotton, wool, and silk, and of detergents for soap. An example of the latter is the replacement of lumber and steel by aluminum for building and packaging materials.

Natural fibers depend ultimately on a renewable energy resource, sunlight, whereas the synthetics rely on fossil fuel derivatives for their manufacture. Unlike the natural fibers, which are subject to decay by molds and bacteria, and thus return to enrich the soil, synthetic fibers and polymers are extremely resistant to decay. Synthetics end up either being burned (thus contributing to atmospheric pollution) or accumulating as essentially nondestructible rubbish (contributing to environmental degradation).

Plastic packages and containers, aluminum cans, artificial fertilizers, synthetic pesticides, detergents—the consequences are similar in each case. They consume energy when they are made, and they damage the environment after they have been used. Technological gains bring economic benefits but are accompanied by severe social and environmental costs. Whether these sorts of penalties are inevitable concomitants of growth or whether the fault lies in the kind of growth will be discussed later in this chapter.

Another distinguishing characteristic of the post-World War II growth period is the steady per capita increase in energy consumption. The substitution of other forms of energy for human toil and their use in providing new goods and services have been hallmarks of the entire industrial period. But in recent decades the rapid acceleration of energy consumption has assumed special importance.

Growth and Energy

The energy crisis of the 1970s is graphically displayed in the supply and demand curves of *Figure 4*. The lower curve shows the estimated total U.S. energy supply from domestic sources for the next 15 years; the upper curve shows projected U.S. demand. Both lines grow wider with time, reflecting the uncertainty of future estimates of both supply and demand. The main uncertainties with regard to supply are prices, government policies, citizen attitudes toward huge energy-supply projects, and possible technological breakthroughs such as large-scale nuclear fusion (in the more distant future). Major uncertainties concerning demand are conservation efforts, governmental policies, and the rate of economic growth. *Figure 4* represents a composite of estimates from responsible sources; nevertheless, because of the factors mentioned above, uncertainties could be even greater than indicated on this graph.

The U.S. energy problem is exhibited by the disparity between the projected supply of energy available from domestic sources and the far greater projected demands (as indicated in *Figure 4* by the space between the two curves and the width of the uncertainty regions). Even with the lowest reasonable energy demand and the highest reasonable supply, there remains a gap that must be filled by purchases of foreign oil. That dependence in itself would not be a problem in a free world economy, provided that the U.S. had goods and services of comparable

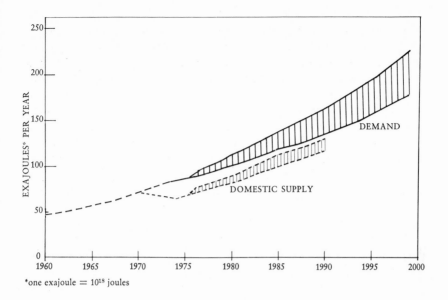

*one exajoule = 10^{18} joules

Figure 4. Total U.S. energy supply and demand projections 1975-90. (Shaded areas indicate the range between available estimates.)

value to sell abroad. However, the oil-producing nations of the world have been able to set up and maintain monopoly prices, and the U.S. must be concerned about maintaining a reasonable balance of trade. The security and stability of oil supplies, the growing political and economic competition for oil, and potentially intolerable balance-of-payments deficits are all critical factors influencing U.S. policy. Estimates of the extent of our dependence on foreign oil vary over a wide range, but we are talking about future oil imports on the order of five to ten million barrels *per day*—at a minimum. To avoid huge balance-of-payments deficits, the nation's energy agencies propose to develop domestic energy sources at an unprecedented rate.

Studies of the U.S. energy situation tend to concur that through at least 1985-90 most of any new domestic energy capacity will have to come from some combination of three sources—coal (including coal-derived liquid and gaseous fuels), offshore oil, and nuclear fission. All three of these sources require tremendous amounts of capital for their development, and all three are likely to encounter continued public opposition on environmental and safety grounds.

U.S. coal is abundant, and the technology already exists to exploit much of it. If annual coal production could be doubled in ten years, to around a billion tons, coal could supply close to a quarter of the estimated annual energy demand of 100-plus exajoules* by 1985. However, doubling coal production would require capital investments involving tens of billions of dollars, expanded transportation systems, expropriation of scarce water supplies in the West for processing, prodigious environmental protection measures, and public acceptance of widespread strip mining.

The potential availability of offshore oil is uncertain, as is the persistence and extent of environmentalist opposition to its development. However, the total petroleum production in the lower 48 states has leveled off to around 11 million barrels per day—slightly over 20 percent of the projected energy demand in 1985. Thus, from these figures, the probable contribution of new offshore oil can be expected at best to fill a small percentage of the 1985 energy demand. (The Alaska pipeline will contribute around 4 percent.)

A number of nuclear fission power plants have been deferred or canceled due to public opposition and concern over safety and environmental impact. The serious problems of adequate safeguards and of disposing of radioactive waste, and the possibility of fissionable materials getting into the hands of terrorists, have raised serious questions as to whether further expansion of nuclear fission technology is a wise course to pursue. Thus continued (or even stronger) public opposition may severely limit the contribution of nuclear power in fulfilling energy demands. Despite earlier and much larger estimates, it now appears that nuclear power cannot be counted on to supply more than about 10 percent of the projected energy demand by 1985.

For the longer term there has been much wishful thinking about other sources of energy. Controlled nuclear fusion is attractive in theory, but we do not know when it will be available, how expensive it will be, or whether it can be made "clean" in terms of radiation hazards. Solar energy for heating and cooling on a local basis (from individual home to community use) appears to be a neglected resource. However, even if it is developed vigorously, such solar power will supply only a minute fraction of projected U.S. energy demand through the end of the century. Large capacity solar power plants are planned eventually, but again the fractional contribution will be small and many years in the future. The most optimistic official estimates propose that by the year 2020 solar power (including that from windmills and utilization of ocean currents and organic combustibles) may be providing a quarter of the total energy used in the U.S.—but it is not clear that anybody believes that estimate is realistic. Geothermal and hydroelectric energy

* One exajoule = 10^{18} joules, slightly under one quadrillion (10^{15}) Btus. If that means nothing to you, 100 exajoules per year amounts to using energy at the rate of roughly 50 million barrels of oil per day.

sources together can supply only a small percentage of the projected U.S. demand by the end of the century.

It becomes clear that environmental, social, and political problems arise in obtaining energy, and again in using it. Obviously the problems would be alleviated by reducing energy demand. Projections of future energy demand are, in essence, based on three assumptions:

1. An assumed rate of growth in the Gross National Product (GNP).
2. An assumed relationship between GNP and energy usage.
3. An assumed potential for energy conservation.

The first assumption confronts us again with the issue of economic growth. The second and third raise important questions about the future structure of our industrial economy.

Since World War II GNP and energy usage have grown proportionally (as shown in *Figure 5*). The correlation is so close it suggests that major cutbacks in energy consumption would reduce GNP (hence, economic prosperity and employment) as well as productivity. Energy cutbacks resulting in lower productivity would also reduce our material

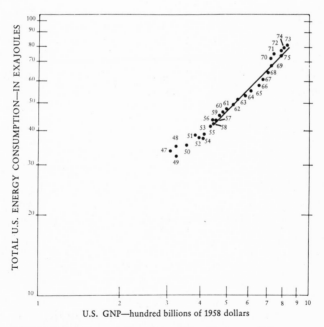

SOURCE: National Economic Research Association; U.S. Bureau of Mines.

Figure 5. Relationship of total annual energy consumption to GNP in the U.S., 1947–75.

standard of living and would weaken the U.S. competitive position in world markets. The reason for the high correlation between energy use and productivity (as measured by GNP) is rather apparent. Productivity in industrial society has been achieved largely by replacing human labor with energy-driven machines; GNP is mainly disposable income—which goes to buy food, clothing, housing, transportation, durable goods, and various services, all of which tend to consume energy in one form or another.

But what is the potential for energy conservation? Is it possible to reduce energy usage through conservation without economic impairment? To some extent, yes. Significant energy savings appear to be possible in a number of areas, including:

- Shift to smaller cars with less power equipment.
- Improved gas mileage of automobile engines.
- Improved efficiency of industrial processes.
- Better insulation and more efficient heating and cooling systems in residences and office buildings.
- Higher efficiency in household appliances (e.g., washing machines, dishwashers).
- Changed transportation patterns (e.g., increased use of car pools, mass transit).
- Changed freight-hauling patterns (e.g., increased use of railways).

Such measures should be taken as far as practicable; wasted energy should be saved. But energy conservation in this sense does not get to the heart of the matter.

In the decade from 1965 to 1975, U.S. energy usage rose an average of about 4.5 percent per year; at this rate energy usage doubles every 16 years. Now suppose that during the decade 1975-85 energy conservation measures save enough wasted energy so that the demand in 1985 is only 75 percent of what was projected for that year. That 25 percent saving would stretch out the doubling time to 23 years. But the critical point is that the demand would still double. And double again. So energy conservation in the conventional sense of the term only buys time; it does not avoid the fundamental problem of endlessly rising demand.

Redefining Productivity

Of course, it is possible to reduce the growth rate of energy demand—to make it zero or even negative. Such a reduction of the energy growth rate has been seriously proposed (e.g., by the Ford Foundation Energy Policy Project in 1974), and we need to examine what it would imply in terms of costs and necessary structural changes. Consider the possibility of restructuring various sectors of society to be more frugal in their use of energy. (The word frugal is used here to connote not austerity but using resources sparingly and wisely.) Here are some of the kinds of measures that could lead toward an energy-frugal society:

1. Reduce agriculture's dependence on fossil fuel derivatives by using less mechanized equipment and less fertilizer; disperse farming to place products closer to consumers; reduce processing and energy-wasteful packaging of food.

2. Reduce industrial consumption of energy by producing more durable, repairable goods (eliminating planned obsolescence), by designing for materials recycling, by altering production processes so that waste heat and materials from one process become inputs to another; change the product mix of the economy to include less energy-consumptive materials and services; disperse manufacturing to produce goods closer to raw materials sources and to users; emphasize craftsmanship and aesthetic quality rather than quantity of goods; emphasize sophisticated but frugal technology (e.g., the integrated-circuit hand calculator).

3. Reduce personal energy requirements by dispersing population to reduce transportation needs from residence to place of work, by increasing dependence on communication instead of transportation (utilizing electronic communications and miniaturized information processing systems), by curbing consumption of energy-intensive goods and services, and by stimulating community-based recreation instead of long-distance travel.

4. Redesign communities to be more self-sufficient and better suited to the environment and ecology, while using sophisticated technology to support highly civilized living conditions, not primitive privation (e.g., by using local solar heating, by employing intensive organic agricultural methods for food production, by reducing requirements for transportation).

A glance at this list emphasizes the drastic changes in consumption habits, industrial structure, social institutions, personal values, and national goals that are implied by real energy frugality. These steps are very different from the earlier list of "energy-saving" or "conservation" measures, which assume that essentially the same goods and services are to be provided as exist today and the same appetites catered to, with only the elimination of unnecessary energy expenditures. By contrast, the energy-frugal measures would require a radical restructuring of institutions and major changes in behavior patterns. Furthermore, they would tend to have a recessive effect on the economy.

Thus, there should be little wonder that proposals to limit growth and reduce productivity usually elicit a negative response. Yet to some extent the negative reaction stems from misconceptions regarding the words *growth* and *productivity*. There can be little doubt that there are indeed limits to uninhibited growth if by the term we mean increasing output of energy-extravagant, materials-extravagant, environmentally destructive goods and services. If we define growth more broadly, however—if we think of growth in human rather than material terms—the possibilities are unlimited. As individuals we experience a profound change in the nature of personal growth during a lifetime. We grow physically for close to 20 years; then that kind of growth ceases. But not all forms of growth stop; indeed the most important growth, intellectual and spiritual, may continue throughout life. Similarly, we can think in terms of societal growth changing its form rather than stopping.

Just as part of our conceptual problem lies in the way we think about growth, our definition of productivity is faulty as well. The usual definition focuses on production per man-hour, which made good sense when labor was a determining factor in production. But for some time now we have been experiencing a labor surplus because of the fantastic rise in labor productivity. Accordingly, the emphasis on productivity per man-hour must shift. Productivity is more properly defined as the ratio of output to all the factors comprising its input (including not only labor but also land, capital, materials, and energy). If the last four factors are of concern because some or all of them are expensive or in short supply, it may be advantageous to increase the investment in labor to reduce the amount of the other factors required.

Another flaw in the conventional measure of productivity lies in defining output in monetary terms. This measure makes no distinction between nourishing and junk foods, durable homeware and plastic throwaways, necessary services and wasteful extravagance. In spite of the positive connotations of the term, productivity is not a suitable measure of the ability of the economy to serve human and social needs. In fact, the hallmark of advanced industrial society has been the tendency for productiveness in human terms to diminish even while economic productivity rises.

Modern agricultural methods offer a classic example of overemphasis on economic productivity. As noted earlier, energy from the sun is becoming a smaller and smaller fraction of the total energy going into food on the table. In narrow economic terms, extravagant use of energy to raise agricultural productivity makes sense—so too does the fact that much of the best farmland has disappeared under subdivisions and shopping centers. But from the societal and humanistic viewpoint it would be more productive (in an expanded sense of the word) if these trends could be reversed—if viability could be returned to the small farm, using energy-frugal but effective agricultural tools, selling unpackaged produce nearby, and providing its operators with a wholesome life close to nature while utilizing the very best small-scale but sophisticated agricultural and domestic technology that human ingenuity can offer. This objective (which is *not* going back to the primitive farm of our ancestors) implies a somewhat more labor-intensive agriculture. But in a period when there is both high unemployment and a renewed appreciation of man's kinship with nature, such farming offers opportunities for human fulfillment.

It is important to remind ourselves that there is no need, ever, for a society to limit productiveness and growth in human terms. As Erich Fromm expresses it in *Man for Himself*, "Productiveness is man's ability to use his powers and to realize the potentialities inherent in him." The resolution of the growth dilemma lies in the creation of a society which is highly productive in human terms, which fosters individual growth and development, but which is also frugal of material resources. A guiding principle is "do more with less." In a frugal society:

- An ethic of frugality and ecological harmony would replace the consumption-and-waste ethic of industrial society.
- Human energy and social resources would be devoted largely to creating meaningful individual lives and a humane society, and far less to those kinds of technological achievements that are wasteful of physical resources.
- Evolutionary change would occur, but growth in a material sense would be slow.
- Technology would be very sophisticated but would conserve energy and materials and would be small in scale.
- Production units (e.g., farms, factories) would tend to be small and relatively self-sufficient.

Accordingly, a frugal society would provide a third alternative to being either underdeveloped or overindustrialized. However, as the next chapter will make clear, the feasibility of the creation of such a society depends upon successful resolution of a dilemma involving the human need for meaningful work—for there must be some other operative measures of human worth in the society to augment or replace goods production and acquisition.

Working Men by F. W. Seiwert

CHAPTER FOUR

THE WORK-ROLES DILEMMA

IF MODERN, INDUSTRIALIZED NATIONS continue in the growth patterns of the past, they will inevitably experience worsening growth-related problems: energy and materials shortages, environmental degradations, shortsighted land-use practices, and endangering of basic life-support systems. If, on the other hand, economic growth slows down for any reason, a whole group of work-related problems will be exacerbated, including unemployment and the threat of unemployment, the economic and social costs of vast welfare systems, poverty and malnutrition amid affluence, widespread underemployment and attendant work dissatisfaction, and discontent among the young and the aging (the former kept out and the latter pushed out of the work force). All of these problems would be less demanding if there were no brakes on economic growth. Thus, in a way, the work-roles dilemma is the reverse side of the growth dilemma. The work-roles dilemma characteristic of advanced industrialized societies reflects a fundamental inability to provide enough satisfying work roles to meet the needs and expectations of the citizenry.

Fear of advancing technology eliminating jobs is far from a new development. Basically the thrust of industrial and technological development over the past two centuries has been to substitute energy-driven equipment for human labor, thus eliminating jobs. But new products and services were continually being generated, thereby creating new jobs as old ones disappeared. In recent decades massive advertising promoting consumption and waste has been needed to create sufficient demand for these new products and services. Now, however, we are encountering environmental and resource limitations that push us in the opposite direction, toward conservation and frugality. Out of this clash of opposing forces arise increasingly intolerable tradeoffs. Although it has been possible to conceal the tendency toward increased unemployment for some time, the problem of "superfluous people" grows more serious as the society becomes more highly industrialized.

As far back as 1930, John Maynard Keynes warned in his *Essays in Persuasion*, "If the economic problem [the struggle for subsistence] is solved, mankind will be deprived of its traditional purpose. . . . Thus for the first time since his creation man will be faced with his real, his permanent problem—how to use his freedom from pressing economic cares. . . . There is no country and no people, I think, who can look forward to the age of leisure and abundance without a dread. . . . It is a fearful problem for the ordinary person, with no special talents to occupy himself, especially if he no longer has roots to the soil or in custom or in the beloved conventions of a traditional society."

Unemployment and Underemployment

It is clear that unemployment is not solely an economic problem. If it were, we could solve the problem merely by establishing some sort of economic redistribution system; the exact form of income maintenance would be a relatively minor issue. But the dilemma is much more fundamental: Unemployment is a psychological and cultural problem as well as an economic one. It involves growing numbers of people who are unwillingly placed outside the mainstream of society, who have little or nothing to contribute to the primary activities of society, and who must come to perceive themselves as superfluous. In a modern society where productiveness comes from one's position in a productive organism, the individual without the organization is unproductive and ineffective; unemployment and underemployment endanger effective citizenship and self-respect. Welfare or income maintenance, or being kept as a pet in any other guise, cannot solve the problem because it does not deal with the psychological consequences of unemployment.

The situation is not much better for the underemployed, whose best work opportunities represent a sorry use of their capabilities. Underemployment—working at less than one's full productive capacity—is common not only in highly industrialized societies, but also in developing societies where a traditional structure has been overrun by the juggernaut of modern industrialism. We must be careful, of course, not to romanticize these nonindustrial societies; no doubt there are many underemployed among peasants around the world. But that is not the point. Underemployment is partly related to education; in fact, the claim has been made that it is the same as overeducation. Having educated its citizens to fuller awareness of their potentialities, a society is in trouble if it does not provide for the exercise of those capabilities.

How Many Are Affected?

It is difficult to determine exactly how many Americans are unemployed and underemployed. Official unemployment figures of 5 or 6 percent or even 8 or 9 percent do not sound too bad. But when researchers have attempted to estimate true unemployment more accurately (taking into account nonworking women who desire jobs, the young and the elderly who are squeezed out of the job market, the despairing who no longer seek work, those who are quite clearly in a featherbedding or make-work situation, and those in "holding institutions" such as reform schools and mental institutions) their figures range from 25 to 35 percent of the potential work force.

It is well known that black and brown minorities are overrepresented in the ranks of the unemployed and underemployed. In 1971 the Senate Subcommittee on Employment, Manpower, and Poverty found that in a number of cities the fraction of the available work force unemployed or earning less than the official poverty-level wage exceeded 40 percent. Most of these individuals were Black, Chicano, or Puerto Rican.

Women, too, make up more than their fair share of the underemployed. More than 90 percent of all receptionists, secretaries, telephone operators, and seamstresses are women. Typically, their educational qualifications far exceed the demands of their jobs. Thus it is not surprising that survey data show that women (along with young Blacks) are among the most dissatisfied in the work force.

Society's underlying anxiety about jobs shows up in pressures on older employees to get out of the work force by retiring early, in inflated age and educational criteria for job entry, in delayed automation of routine operations, and in subtle forms of featherbedding (such as regulations that force trucks and taxicabs to make return trips empty). This anxiety is apparent whenever there is talk about canceling a defense contract or space project; it becomes a political force affecting such issues as energy conservation, pollution control, and land use–where actions that are desirable from other standpoints are ruled out because they would cost jobs.

If it is difficult to measure unemployment and underemployment accurately, it is far more difficult to assess what it means in human terms for a large fraction of the nation's adult population to feel unneeded. Employment (including such unpaid positions as student or housewife) is symbolic of having a place in the social order. Excluded from full and valued participation are the elderly, the young, the unemployables, and those who are performing useless make-work and know it. All of them are deprived of the self-esteem that comes from having a social role that others judge to be useful. As a consequence of wasting their human potential, these people often develop such pathologies as chronic life disorganization, listlessness, family instability, mental depression, alcoholism, drug abuse, or other self-destructive or antisocial behavior.

There are other social costs, also difficult to calculate. The main barrier to successful education of disadvantaged children appears to be the absence of a realistic opportunity for satisfying employment. Fear of unemployment seems to be a root cause of racial and intergroup conflict. Unemployment is clearly an important factor in crime and delinquency. The specter of expanding joblessness weakens efforts to improve the quality of life, preserve the natural environment, conserve scarce resources, attain more equitable distribution of income, create a more workable world economy, and reduce war-spawning tensions between rich and poor nations. Resolution of the employment problem seems clearly to be the linchpin prerequisite for rendering a number of other societal problems resolvable.

Trends and Prognosis

A look to the future is not reassuring. The work force of tomorrow will be better educated than that of today. Its expectations will undoubtedly be higher and its values different. We noted in Chapter Two that survey data compiled by Daniel Yankelovich indicate value shifts among workers (toward greater concern for the quality of life and values grounded in a "New Naturalism"), with the young and well educated leading the pack. The average age of the work force will be shifting downward for the next 15 years. By 1980 one in four American workers will have a college degree; half of these college-educated workers will be under 35, while half of all the workers with only an elementary school education will be over the age of 50. More workers will be in white-collar jobs, but these can be as stultifying, repetitive, and unchallenging as blue-collar work.

Demographic data tell part of the reason why the problem of worker alienation is real, of lasting duration, and built into the basic structure of the society. In the late 1960s in the U.S. two basic demographic lines crossed. There are now more people in the adult labor force with at least one year of college than there are higher-level jobs to absorb them.

The proportion of the adult labor force with one or more years of college rose from 19 percent in 1960 to 27 percent in 1970. But the proportion of total employment represented by managerial, administrative, technical, and professional jobs was rising more slowly; it went from 20 percent in 1960 to only 22 percent in 1970. In sum, more of the work force will be better educated and will be making more demands for interesting and meaningful jobs that satisfy their requirements for challenge, growth, and self-fulfillment but will become disaffected because too few fulfilling jobs will be available.

The myth of education as a sure route to increased status, power, and income has been exploded. It is estimated that from two to three million college graduates will be competing for blue-collar jobs during the next decade. Women are entering the work force in increasing numbers and they tend toward white-collar work. One effect of this growing pool of highly qualified workers has been inflation of educational criteria for jobs, so that a high school diploma is required to bag groceries or to perform unskilled labor. This practice has contributed to dissatisfaction among the overqualified workers and has simultaneously raised higher job barriers for the poor, the uneducated, and the young.

These problems are not restricted to the capitalist democracies. Worker unrest and organizational ineffectiveness are common in socialist and communist countries. The problems seem to be deeply rooted in the structure of technologically advanced societies. Although the more pressing problems of inflation and unemployment may push the issue of worker dissatisfaction off the front page, this problem seems destined to be a major concern of developed societies for the indefinite future.

Neither manpower training programs nor broader education, by themselves, provide the answer to the employment dilemma of modern society. Additional education, rather than increasing productivity and job satisfaction, tends to have a negative effect on both when people are unable to find work that makes use of their enhanced training and ability.

But statistics on education and work fail to get at the heart of the underemployment issue. One is reminded of the two medieval stonecutters who were working on the same project. Asked what he was doing, one answered, "I'm squaring up this bloody stone." The other replied, "I am building a cathedral." The first was underemployed; the second was not. Is underemployment, then, a cultural artifact or a state of mind?

Clearly what counts is not so much *what* work a person does, but *what he perceives he is doing it for*. The frontiersman, the old-time craftsman, the farmer blessed with a fine piece of land all would have scoffed at the idea that they were underemployed. But once mechanized agriculture appeared on the scene, one could no longer follow a horse with a plow in the same spirit as before. When people speak of "meaningful work" they do not mean that the task itself is necessarily exciting and challenging every moment, but rather that the larger project of which it is a part has meaning.

Thus the work-roles dilemma clearly relates to what has been called by sociologist Amatai Etzioni the "central project" of a society. If there is a central project in which people believe—such as conquering the Western frontier or the technological frontier, or building a new society or a world democratic order—then even routine tasks take on meaning. On the other hand, if there is no central project that enlists the loyalties and commitments of the citizens, even a technically complex and challenging task can become stultifying and meaningless.

Basic Types of Work

To see how fundamental this dilemma is, let's look at it in another way. Mortimer Adler, in *The Capitalist Manifesto*, suggests four classifications of work. From the individual's standpoint there is work that tends to be instrumental—intrinsically unrewarding, mechanical in quality, undertaken because of the need for subsistence. At the opposite extreme is work that is intrinsically rewarding and creative in quality. From society's standpoint there are also two important categories of work. One is work that is sustaining for society and productive of wealth—the necessities, comforts, and conveniences of life. At the other extreme is work that benefits the human spirit and civilization, thereby enhancing the quality of life. Thus, there are four general types of work:

1. Instrumental for the individual, sustaining for society (e.g., mechanical and routine labor of industrial production).

2. Instrumental for the individual, civilizing for society (e.g., research or clerical assistance to scientific or artistic endeavors).

3. Creative for the individual, sustaining for society (e.g., creative work of technicians, managers, physicians).

4. Creative for the individual, civilizing for society (e.g., creative work of pure scientists, artists).

Admittedly it would be difficult to be very precise in this classification of work, but recognition of these broadly defined work types will aid our discussion of the work-roles dilemma. At most times in most so-

The Changing West by Thomas Hart Benton

cieties, work has been predominantly sustaining as far as the society was concerned. Only a fraction of the society's efforts could be spared for civilizing, life-enhancing activities. Following the Industrial Revolution, as technology, wealth, and education increased, there tended to be less need for instrumental-sustaining work—and also less willingness to do it. The development of technology nurtured a great deal of intrinsically rewarding, creative work and increasing educational levels brought more desire for such work.

As the material standard of living increased, the quality of required goods and services rose. Advancing technology in the industrial production of goods and services tended to eliminate vast numbers of routine mechanical jobs, but also to create vast numbers of instrumental-sustaining and creative-sustaining work opportunities. The fraction of the work force involved with primary occupations (in agriculture, lumber, fishing, mining) decreased steadily; that in secondary occupations (goods production) increased for a while but recently began a decline (see *Figure 6*). The fraction in tertiary (services) and quaternary (learning, knowledge industries) is increasing, having gone from around 30 percent in 1890 to around 60 percent in 1968. (During the same period, the part of the work force in professional and technical occupations rose from 4 to 13 percent, making this the most rapidly growing category.) As productivity in the service occupations increases, the segment of the work force employed in services will presumably reach a peak and then decrease, as occurred in agriculture and goods produc-

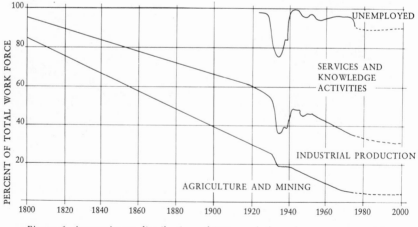

Figure 6. Approximate distribution of U.S. work force by sector, over time.

tion. The total portion of the work force involved with work that is sustaining for society has not changed greatly over the years because society's appetite for sustenance "needs" has continued to rise.

In recent years a profound change has been taking place in this picture, essentially due to society's phenomenal technological and educational successes. The amount of instrumental-sustaining and creative-sustaining work that the economy can provide is being limited on the one hand by environmental and resource constraints and on the other by growing citizen reaction against the consumption-and-waste ethic, planned obsolescence, and the throwaway society. (Remember when the description "throwaway society" had positive connotations of technological progress?) In spite of our almost continual involvement in war or preparations for war, a mammoth aeronautics and space program, and an expanding role as arms supplier to the world, our society seems less and less able to consume all the products required to sustain full employment.

The ultimate resolution of this problem seems clearly to involve large-scale expansion of work opportunities of the types that contribute to the civilizing of society and enhancement of the quality of life. However, strong objections counter any suggestion that such an effort become national policy. Probably the two strongest oppositions are to massive public works projects reminiscent of the Depression years and to "paying for leisure." In partial answer to the first objection, it should be noted that work opportunities need not be structured in the public sector. They can also be in the "third sector" of voluntary associations (e.g., consumer and environmentalist organizations, religious orders, labor unions) and nonprofit institutions (e.g., private schools, foundations, service and research organizations). Neither need these civilizing activities be economically "nonproductive." With regard to the second objection, the society does of course remunerate many persons for performing creative work which they enjoy doing. The political problem of who is selected for these opportunities, and how, is an aspect of income and wealth distribution that we will return to later on in the discussion.

Now we can see more clearly the fundamental perceptual change that will have to precede a resolution of the work dilemma. In a technologically advanced society where production of sufficient goods and services can be handled with ease, *employment exists primarily for self-development, and is only secondarily concerned with the production of goods and services.* This concept of work represents a profound shift in perception, with implications that reverberate throughout the entire social-political-economic system.

The Dual Role of Work

Work, as we have noted, has two functions that are quite distinct—one economic and the other social. The economic function is as a mechanism for income distribution, presumably related to the individual's contribution to the production of needed goods and services. The social function is as a legitimated role in the activities of the society. In this latter role, work is the activity of self-development in the process of contributing to the purposive activities of the larger society.

When society required the services of most of its members to produce needed goods and services, it made sense to think of rewarding individuals according to their direct contribution to that production. But two related aspects of the development of capital-intensive production have rendered that concept obsolete. One is that the relative contribution of labor in industrialized production declines steadily in proportion to contribution of capital. The other is that the fraction of the potential work force directly engaged in production of goods and services is also declining.

Reduction of the importance of labor in production is inherent in industrial development. Each worker can produce more wealth because of the capital-intensive technology available to him. As the industrialization process proceeds, the increases in wealth produced are more and more the result of capital and technological and managerial expertise, and less and less the contribution of routine, narrowly trained, or unskilled labor. Nevertheless, the real wages of mechanical laborers (those whose work could be performed by machines) have risen as fast as, or faster than, the wages of managers and technically creative workers. Thus wage levels as an equitable basis for income distribution become even further divorced from the real value added by the worker.

Reduction of the fraction of the work force involved with industrial production is also an inherent trend as industrialization proceeds. The part of the total work force engaged in primary (agricultural and extractive) and secondary (goods production) occupations has dropped from over 90 percent in 1800 to about 36 percent in 1960 and 29 percent in 1975. Even these figures fail to show the true extent of the drop, for they are buoyed up by the artificial stimulation of consumption from a national growth and full-employment policy, implemented in part by massive defense expenditures, space programs, and arms sales to other nations. As the fraction of persons involved with production goes down, contribution to production becomes less satisfactory as a basis for income distribution.

In reaction to the manifest inadequacies of the concept of distributing income according to productivity, the government role in redistributing income has grown vastly over the past century. Governmental redistribution is accomplished by direct transfer payments, such as social insurance and public assistance programs; by the graduated income tax and other differential monetary and fiscal policies; and by controls on prices, wages, and interest rates. Accordingly, because of such policies, the link between productivity and income has become still weaker. For all practical purposes the notion that an individual's income is determined by the productivity of his labor (plus return from property) has become obsolete. As a substitute, society is confusedly attempting to rationalize income distribution with vaguely defined principles of welfare and equity.

Thus, on one hand, work is the least controversial form of income distribution; yet on the other, in an increasingly industrialized economy, work becomes decreasingly suitable for that purpose. We also see a similar situation with regard to the social function of work. Work is one of the most socially acceptable and one of the most constructive ways for people to occupy the major portion of their waking hours and to play a part in the society's activities. But in the advanced industrial economy, work opportunities become an increasingly scarce commodity. This is the puzzling and fundamental dilemma we face today— the effectiveness of *both* roles of work has deteriorated.

Steps Toward Resolution

We need to look more closely at these two functions in turn to see how the work-roles dilemma could be resolved. As we proceed it would be well to remind ourselves again how fundamentally this dilemma is enmeshed in advanced stages of industrialization. In terms of its own goals of efficiency, labor productivity, and material growth and consumption (achieved through organization and management of work and replacement of human labor by machines), industrialization must be judged an unqualified success. In economic terms, the problem of production seems solved once and for all.

If human beings basically sought to escape from work, industrialization might be considered a success from a social standpoint as well, since it has made possible the elimination of so much work that humans once had to do. But both from observation of worker behavior and from the findings of psychological research, there is ample evidence that persons seek meaningful activity and meaningful relationships. Man thrives not on mindless pleasure, but on challenge. Thus, although full employment is no longer needed from a production standpoint, full participation is essential from a social standpoint.

Only if economic growth is high enough can production of goods and services generate the work roles needed. But consumer demand is not insatiable, and consumers are displaying increasing resistance to attempts to condition them to want all that a full-employment economy can produce. Furthermore, growth is limited by new concerns about the "new scarcity" and social costs. It is part of the nature of industrial development that the process of production will eventually fail to provide enough work roles either for fulfillment of the economic (income-distribution) function of work or the social function.

The kinds of mechanisms that a society chooses for economic distribution depend upon cultural attitudes and values. In the U.S. attitudes have been changing toward the distribution mechanism that economists call *transfer payments*. This term refers to income payments and transfers of purchasing power to people deemed needy or worthy, *without regard to their providing a specific service in return*. Examples of transfer payments are welfare, veterans' pensions, and Medicare. Since the Depression, the U.S. economic strategy has been to promote growth, consumption (and waste), and to manipulate the economy to achieve the fullest employment possible and hence to minimize such transfer payments as unemployment compensation and welfare. Minimizing transfer payments was considered desirable not only for economic reasons, but also because of the deleterious social consequences of most welfare programs. In the 1960s, however, with growing talk of affluent leisure societies, there were signs of a more liberal attitude toward transfer payments (although there remains even today much resistance to the "free handout").

If the economists' usual definition of a transfer payment is broadened to include *transfers from institutions and individuals as well as from governments*, we note that there are at least four distinct kinds of transfer payments:

1. Those based on membership, in which a person is entitled to support simply by virtue of belonging to a particular group—the family, community, organization, or society (e.g., transfers to wives, children, students, commune members).

2. Those which are a social investment, based on promise (e.g., some research grants, competitive scholarships).

3. Those based on need, but conditional (e.g., some scholarships, Local Initiatives Programs in Canada wherein unemployed individuals must propose and carry out socially constructive tasks to qualify for payments).

4. Those based on need, but otherwise unconditional (e.g., welfare and unemployment payments, assistance to the aged).

Using this broadened definition, if all four types of payments are included, more than 60 percent of the population (mostly housewives, children, and students) are already supported wholly or in part by transfer payments. All but 5 percent fit into one of the first three types; nevertheless, the negative aspects of the fourth type tend to give undesirable connotations to income transfers in general.

Some aspects of the work-roles problem could be alleviated by greatly expanding the number of transfer payments available to the second and third categories. Because these two types comprise such a small percentage of all transfer payments, the numbers involved could be multiplied many times without appreciably increasing the overall percentage. However, there is a problem. The kinds of persons who could qualify for these two types of transfer payments have abilities that would fit them for existing roles in the economy without such transfers. Conversely, those most in need of employment opportunity, those who find it hardest to place themselves in the industrial economy, would also tend to be those least able to devise their own socially constructive work activities if they were offered transfer payments of the second or third type.

There is, however, a way around this difficulty. Imagine that we possess some means of assessing people's capability for self-definition —that is, the ability to choose among available social roles or invent new ones, to move toward self-selected goals, to select and actualize their own potential abilities. Some individuals would rank high in this self-definition ability; they could either find suitable work opportunities or construct their own, becoming entrepreneurs or creative artists or independent consultants, for example. We know such individuals; typically they find many options open to them. They select their own goals and are relatively unconstrained by whatever organizational roles they may play. Most people would fall in the middle of the scale, with a moderate amount of self-defining ability. Such people generally are successful at finding and holding jobs, and their work roles tend to be important components of their self-image or self-definition. Lower on the scale are individuals with meager self-defining ability, capable of doing assigned routine work but exerting little control over their own fate. Let us now look at the transfer-payment mechanism with these three groups in mind.

The first group—people who have a high self-definition capability—

does not require our attention. They can and will take care of themselves. The second group contains many persons who would like to change roles—to extend their education, shift careers, make some voluntary response to societal needs—but who, because of family or other responsibilities, feel unable to break free. They have jobs, but would like some temporary income maintenance to facilitate a change in roles, or possibly more lasting income maintenance to make possible some alternative constructive activity. In the third group are many persons who are maintained by some sort of welfare program but desire structured jobs to help them with their problem of self-definition. They have income maintenance but want jobs.

Once the work-roles problem is formulated in this way, we see one of the essential characteristics of its resolution. The needed trick is to provide more income maintenance for the second group, to enable them to move *out* of the more structured jobs to allow room for members of the third group. Instead of the present situation in which there are structured jobs for people with moderate self-defining ability and income maintenance for the unemployed (who tend to be low in self-defining ability), the reverse would make far more sense. Those who want and need structured work opportunities should have jobs. Those who would give up unchallenging jobs if income maintenance were available to free them for other activity should have that opportunity, thus making positions free for the former group. This direction is the one that must be taken if resolution is to be found for *both* the unemployment and underemployment problems endemic to advanced industrialization.

The term *enhancement income maintenance* seems appropriate for this latter form of aid, to distinguish it from the *subsistence income maintenance* that will always be required for those who are not able to function in the economic structure in any other way—whether because of disability or other reasons. The purpose of enhancement income maintenance would be to provide support, on either a temporary or a lasting basis, for those who have demonstrated ability to hold structured jobs but who want to carry out some project of manifest social value. Such activities could include study and research (now generally provided for only an elite few through scholarships and fellowships), providing educational opportunities for others, preserving and beautifying the environment, carrying out a social experiment, assisting the handicapped, creating in art or music, writing, providing companionship for the young or aged. Funds for individuals or for group projects would need to be available on a competitive basis to keep incentive levels up. Preferably, the funding would be from diverse sources in public, private, and voluntary/nonprofit sectors.

With enhancement income maintenance as a key concept, we now see that there *is* a direction the society could take that would improve the effectiveness with which *both* the economic and the social functions of work are carried out. Resolution of the work-roles dilemma will require that private business and government supplement normal employment with several components:

1. Enhancement income maintenance, facilitating self-initiated, intrinsically rewarding work opportunities and simultaneously increasing mobility in the job structure, as described above.

2. Public works projects and public service employment, to accomplish socially desirable objectives when it is not feasible to have these activities carried out in the private or "third (voluntary) sector."

3. Subsistence income maintenance as needed for those unable to function in the economy in any other way.

4. Universal unemployment insurance, consisting of base-level income maintenance plus a tapering-down supplement, depending on one's annual income at the time of disemployment, to reduce the shock of sudden unemployment (and, by its existence, to reduce pervasive and unwholesome anxiety over the possibility of unemployment).

These proposed suggestions should be considered in the context of the possible transformation to a transindustrial society. The dilemmas of industrial society are fundamental ones and, as we shall reiterate many times, probably require major whole-system changes for their resolution. Fragments of the transformation examined in isolation may appear impractical. The solution to the work-roles dilemma described above would be workable only if society were deeply committed to many of the principles we have foreseen as components of an emerging transindustrial society.

Hooded Beggarwoman by Ernst Barlach

CHAPTER FIVE

THE WORLD DISTRIBUTION DILEMMA

A THIRD DILEMMA confronts the technologically and industrially advanced world: We cannot risk the international instability that results from the vast disparities between the rich and poor nations, yet neither of the obvious solutions—making the poor nations richer or the rich nations poorer—seems feasible. The world probably cannot afford to have the gap closed through making the poor nations as productive, consuming, and polluting as the rich nations; at the same time, the rich nations are not likely to choose voluntarily to become less materialistic and more frugal.

As the nonindustrialized nations modernize and begin to demand their share of scarce resources (including minerals and fossil fuels) and as the poorest nations are devastated by famine and plague while consumption levels continue to rise in the advanced industrial nations, the distribution dilemma will become a major force shaping world events. A markedly improved standard of living for the world's nearly three billion poor does not appear possible without continued economic growth on the part of both developing and developed nations; yet, that very growth poses an undeniable threat to the environment and to the health of man. In view of the signs of overload already appearing, it becomes clear that for the masses of the world to reach anything like the living standard of the 6 percent of the world population living in the U.S. (who consume a third of the resources and spew out half the world's nonorganic waste) would strain the planet's carrying capacity. The expectations and demands of the developing nations may well rise at such a pace that they could not be met even with a drastic lowering of the material standard of living in the rich nations. Yet if the rising expectations are not met, the likelihood of accelerating world instability seems high.

No single characteristic of the world as it has been shaped by the industrial era stands out so clearly as the coexistence of mass hunger alongside wasteful abundance for the few. No other aspect of society is so fraught with hazard for the future. Robert Heilbroner, in *An Inquiry Into the Human Prospect*, pointed out "the ghastly resemblance of the world's present economic condition to an immense train, in which a few passengers, mainly in the advanced capitalist world, ride in first-class coaches, in conditions of comfort unimaginable to the enormously greater numbers crammed into the cattle cars that make up the rest of the train's carriages. . . . [To the underdeveloped world] the passengers in the first-class coaches not only ride at their ease but have decorated their compartments and enriched their lives by using the work and appropriating the resources of the masses who ride behind them."

Disparities between rich and poor nations are not new, of course. Several things *are* new, however. One development is that communications media now reach the poor masses and continually remind them of the disparities. Another is the worldwide revolution of rising expectations and the mood of self-determination that is replacing the attitude of submission among those who view themselves as oppressed. A third development is the increasing vulnerability of our complex society to disruption. The elements of society are so closely coupled that damage to one halts the activity of many elements, thus making it possible for small dissident groups to apply pressures, through terrorism and sabotage, far greater than those they could muster politically or economically. We must face the possibility that threats to the world industrial system, ranging from raw material embargoes to nuclear blackmail, may be used to force the industrially developed world to transfer large amounts of wealth to the poverty-stricken world. Such actions become a credible eventuality precisely because they may be the only way that poor nations feel that they can hope to remedy their condition.

Population and GNP

Most of the world's population is poor. Roughly 70 percent of the human family live in nonindustrialized countries characterized by conditions of desperate poverty. The other 30 percent live in developed countries with advanced, essentially stable economies and rising levels of affluence unique in the history of man. The disparity between the developed and the developing nations is real, profound, and many-dimensioned. In most instances there is little social or economic middle ground between rich and poor. The two populations differ greatly in such areas as income, literacy, nutrition, urbanization, industrialization, technological achievement, and patterns of consumption.

GNP per capita is generally accepted as one of the best available measures of a country's wealth or poverty. Over two-thirds of the world's people live in countries with a per capita GNP of less than $500; only 11 percent live in countries with a per capita GNP of over $3,500. (The per capita GNP in the U.S. in 1974 exceeded $5,500.) The United States, with only 8.5 percent of the total population of the free-market economies, produces almost 45 percent of the total GNP of the non-Communist world. The industrially developed countries, whether their economies are planned or free, contain less than 30 percent of the world population but produce approximately 85 percent of gross world product.

The gap between the rich and poor nations continues to widen because the population in the poor countries is growing much faster and their economic bases are so much lower. During the 1960s economic growth rates were around 4 percent in the industrially developed countries and 5.5 percent in developing nations. Per capita GNP, however, went up at an annual rate of 3.7 percent in industrially developed countries and only 3 percent on the average in developing countries. Rich countries enjoyed a per capita GNP increase of $300 over the decade, whereas the poor countries realized only a $10 increase.

Internal Disparities

The vast disparity of income and wealth *within* the poor countries contributes to their problem. Virtually all of the developing countries are characterized by what has been called a dual economy—two populations in the same nation with entirely different patterns of living. In the Latin American countries the wealthiest 5 percent of the population garner about 30 percent of the income, whereas the poorest 20 percent receive only about 3 to 4 percent of the total. In the poor countries of Asia and Africa the situation is even more extreme—the wealthiest 5 percent receive as much as 50 percent of the total income. In these nations a small portion of the society is urban, industrial, and modern; the remainder of the population is either rural, existing according to traditional agricultural patterns, or urban poor, subsisting on scraps from the industrial and commercial segment.

Attempts to modernize a nation's economy usually widen the internal gap between the rich and poor. Successful industrial development in the cities tends to destroy the rural economic structure. Introduction of modern agricultural methods deprives peasants of their livelihood. Together these two effects cause mass migration into the cities, adding to urban problems, thus making the cities unmanageable. Modern public health measures such as sanitation, swamp drainage, and pest control reduce rural death rates, increase the population, and add further to the unemployable surplus of manpower.

The internal disparities between rich and poor are as much political as economic, involving as much a variance in self-image as in material welfare. Development in nonindustrial societies requires that the poor overcome not only hunger and material deprivation, but ignorance, feelings of inferiority, powerlessness, and subjection as well. It involves their achieving emancipation from the status of mere subjects, participation in both economic production and effective government, awareness of the principles guiding social organization, and a free, enriching, and responsible relationship with their material and social environment. The barriers to the achievement of such measures are of awesome proportions.

Interdependent Characteristics

Many of the poor countries are so trapped in self-perpetuating stagnation that the outlook seems almost hopeless. Characteristics common to such countries appear to be both cause and effect:

- Primitive agriculture (involving a high proportion of the labor force).
- Inefficient industrialization and low labor productivity.
- Low income levels and a low material standard of living.
- Chronic unemployment and underemployment.
- Deficient transportation and communication.
- Low levels of literacy, education, and scientific and technological knowledge.
- Chronic nutritional deficiencies, widespread health problems, and limited health care.
- High rates of population growth.
- Low levels of saving and investment, and limited accumulation of capital.
- Excessive dependence on foreign trade and capital.
- Underutilization of natural resources.
- Coexistence of modern and primitive economic sectors.

These features are so interdependent that the improvement of any requires the changing of all; the problems of one area magnify those in the others. Inefficient industrialization and low productivity produce a low material standard of living, which leaves little margin for savings and the production of capital. Imported capital is of limited usefulness because of poor transportation and communication, the inefficient labor force, and overwhelming societal problems. Substandard health and education contribute to low productivity, which in turn limits the resources available for health care and education.

Two characteristics in particular play a fundamental role—population and nutrition. If the economic standard of living is to rise at all, obviously the growth rate of disposable income (i.e., GNP) must accelerate more rapidly than population. Population growth depends upon both fertility and mortality. The fertility rate in the industrialized Western world has declined from around 38 births per thousand prior to the Industrial Revolution to about 18 per thousand by the early 1970s; in many developing nations it remains around 40 to 45 births per thousand. In the industrially developed nations, with a higher proportion of older persons, mortality rates are holding constant or increasing slightly; conversely, the higher proportion of young people in underdeveloped countries has contributed to a rapidly declining mortality rate. The net result of these rates of change is that the population in the modern, industrialized countries is increasing at less than 1 percent a year, whereas in the poor, developing nations the annual rate of population growth is around 3 percent.

Thus it follows that the material standard of living improves (i.e., per capita GNP rises) in the industrialized nations whenever total GNP increases at a rate of more than 1 percent per year. In the poor countries, however, a 3 percent increase in total GNP is required just to break even. Rapid population growth also impedes economic growth by placing extra demands on society for education, health care, nutrition, and employment.

Nutritional deficiency, inextricably tied to the rate of population growth, is another fundamental problem in the poorer countries. As global population continues to increase exponentially, it becomes increasingly difficult to maintain a comparable rate of growth in food production. Thus the world now faces the real possibility of a widespread Malthusian catastrophe. Futurists and agronomists alike have warned of the serious possibility of global "mega-famines" by the end of this decade. Even now it is estimated that between 30 and 50 percent of the world's population suffer from malnutrition and 10 to 15 percent from undernourishment. Enormous numbers of human beings are slowly, inexorably dying because they receive too few essential nutrients and have greatly lowered resistance to disease.

As global food scarcities become more and more apparent, so also does the inequitable distribution of available food. It is the populations of the poorest countries that would be decimated by a world food shortage. The food substance of most concern is protein, particularly animal protein. When nations become richer their consumption preferences tend to shift from grains to meat. As a result of changing tastes and the industrialization of meat production, more and more of this is grain-fed meat. Today an increasingly large portion of the world's grain protein is going to animals rather than humans—a dubious practice in view of the fact that it takes from four to 12 pounds of grain protein to produce a single pound of meat protein. But this trend reflects the laws of economics, since the rich can afford more and more beef while the poor can afford less and less cereal.

Both the total protein consumption and the share that is animal protein tend to be much lower in the poor countries than in the rich ones. The daily per capita intake of protein from animal sources is more than ten times as great in North America as in the underdeveloped countries of Asia and Africa. The portion of the diet made up of starchy staples (wheat, rice, potatoes, cassava, etc.) drops from between 55 and 70 percent in agrarian societies to around 20 percent in wealthier industrialized societies.

Protein deficiency has come to be recognized as one of the most serious impediments to development of human potential. The infant mortality rate in some poor countries is as much as five times that in the developed countries, the difference being due almost entirely to nutritional deficiencies, mainly protein. Even when death does not occur, nutritional deficiencies during the critical first few years can cause irreversible brain damage, resulting in severe impairment of mental ability.

Trade, Manpower, and Capital

As has been previously discussed, there is a natural tendency for wealth and power to accumulate in any society—a trend that must be countered in a stable society by cultural or institutional mechanisms. There are no such mechanisms in the world economic system, however. The wealthy nations naturally use their economic and political power to protect and enhance their privileged position. As a result, the developing nations find themselves at a serious disadvantage in various aspects of economic relations among nations—trade, manpower migration, and capital transfers.

Wheat by Thomas Hart Benton

Trade policies consistently discriminate against products imported from poor countries, especially potentially competitive processed goods. Unprocessed commodities typically enter duty free, whereas the same products are subject to tariffs if they have already been processed. This practice keeps the poor countries from taking advantage of their lower labor costs, one of the few resources the poorest of the nations possess; it discourages industrial growth and reinforces the dependence upon industrial nations of countries that supply raw materials. As a result of all these factors, the poor countries' share of total world trade is small and declining. Because they maintain a much greater volume of total trade, rich countries even export more primary resources than the poor countries. The resource-supplying nations are slowly learning to band together for mutual assistance and to use such devices as cartel-controlled pricing. But such a technique only works for nations that control strategic resources in sufficient quantity that they provide an effective bargaining position.

With regard to the migration of human capital, the flow of people goes both ways—technical assistance from the rich countries to the poor and technically skilled labor from the poor nations to the rich. The "brain drain" is serious in only a few developing countries—Iran, Greece, Turkey—but it is a factor in all. Professionally qualified persons are attracted to better opportunities in the rich countries. Meanwhile, unskilled laborers in the poor countries can usually neither migrate nor find work; therefore unemployment and underemployment worsen. Occasionally unskilled workers can enter developed nations as "guest workers," but if a recession occurs they are returned to their home countries where they add to the unemployment problem there.

Monetary aid for the development of poor countries has become a standard facet of the foreign policy of the wealthy nations, particularly since World War II. Military aid has been more easily justified than economic aid; hence economic assistance to a less-developed country has often been contingent upon a military alliance. The conventional argument for developmental assistance has been that it is good for business; it will widen the market for exports, provide new opportunities for private investment, and build sources of supply for imports. The humanitarian argument for aid to the poor has also been effective, not only as a plea for the relief of suffering, but also as a way to strengthen the moral claim of the modern industrialized nations to their positions of superior power. Nevertheless, both the quantity and the quality of aid for economic development have decreased in recent years, even as the income gap between the rich and poor countries has widened.

Is There a Solution?

All the economic disparities between rich and poor, highly visible in a shrinking world, are exerting growing pressure on the international political fabric. The poor nations are becoming more aware of what they regard as their legitimate power (including the political use of violence) and their basic property rights. If the hopes and dreams of the world's poor continue to be frustrated while the rich become steadily richer, prospects for world peace will grow dimmer and "wars of redistribution" will become more likely.

It is important to recognize how deeply the dilemma of inequities in distribution between the rich and the poor is implicated in the development and structure of industrialization. Among man's fundamental needs are food, shelter, relationship to nature, and a meaningful role in society. The precolonial peasant had these needs fulfilled. In the progression through mercantilism and industrialization, food became a commodity, as did human labor and access to land; economic reasoning superseded tradition as a guide to behavior; altered social institutions plus population growth brought a shortage of work roles and the impairment of village social and economic order. In the industrializing countries nonagricultural production rose, the fraction of the working force in agriculture dropped, and per capita and per acre production increased. Conversely, during most of this same period in colonized countries like India, Indonesia, and Vietnam, nonagricultural production dropped, the fraction of the working force in agriculture rose, and per capita and per acre production decreased. The world has always known poverty, but its contemporary form, coexisting with abundance, appears to be inherent to the industrialization process.

The dilemma appears to be unresolvable without fundamental changes in the world economic system and world culture. One blunt fact reveals the rich-poor dilemma in its most fundamental form: The poor are poor because their labor is worthless, they have no ownership stake in the economy, and they lack the political power to change the situation. Their labor is worthless because the industrialized production system has no need for it. They have no stake because ownership of the land and resources has been defined in a way that excludes them. Their lack of political power in the past has been primarily a matter of lack of awareness that acquiescence—in a system that does not value their labor and offers them no stake—is not their only choice. Today that awareness is changing rapidly.

The real disparity is between awakening aspirations and stark realities. Experts can twist statistics to show that economic differences are growing or shrinking, that the poor are better or worse off, but the precise figures are irrelevant. If the aspirations of the poor, whetted by vivid worldwide communication of the disparities between rich and poor, are growing faster than the realities are changing, then the destabilizing gap is growing.

A minimum condition for eventual resolution of the rich-poor dilemma is that two different kinds of paths be opened up. There needs to be a more effective way by which nations that want rapid industrialization can be helped to achieve it. But for those nations who find such a path unattractive, either because they recognize the problems of industrialization or because they do not want to destroy valued traditions, the viability of the society in its nonindustrialized state needs to be assured.

For the option of rapid industrialization to become a reality, a new concept of international economics is required to embody the idea that just as individual nations establish mechanisms for the redistribution of wealth and power, so must the international society. There must be formal and actual recognition of the fact that a prerequisite of world economic and political stability is assurance of some minimum protection for the rights and opportunities of even the weakest members of the society. Now that the earth's population has become a "global village," such protection will be demanded persistently. International mechanisms will undoubtedly include cartels of resource-producing nations, such as OPEC, and federations of developing nations, such as the Andean Community, to countervail the tremendous economic power of the mammoth multinational corporations. Other procedures may include some formalized, dependable system of transferring economic payments from rich to poor nations, which would be justified on the same grounds that transfer payments to the poor and weak are justified within nations.

Whatever specific methods are employed, there must be a modification of the basic structural forces and barriers that keep the poor poor —to counter more effectively the natural tendency for wealth and power to accumulate further where it is already possessed. Acceptance of colonialism as a legitimate system has been withdrawn, whether that colonialism be political and overt or economic and *de facto*.

The need to open up to the nonindustrialized world the option of *not* following the Western industrialized model is less understood. For a long time the concept of material progress through technological and industrial development seemed so irresistible to the modern mind that it was literally inconceivable that any society might, having tasted its fruits, prefer something else. Only in the last decade or so have we begun to listen to the weak voice of the underdeveloped cultures as they have been run over by the great industrial juggernaut, protesting that they too might have attributes worth preserving. Groups in our own society have found rejuvenating meaning in the ways of the American Indian, the peasant, the African tribesman, and the Buddhist monk. China and Southeast Asia have strongly rejected the goals and values of Western-style elite-dominated industrial society, and we have found this rejection particularly baffling. A large segment of humanity has raised a mighty cry that high-technology, industrialized society has not worked to the overall benefit of man.

Changes in the world system need to be devised to strengthen the capacity of local cultures to avoid some of the problems accompanying industrialization, or even to resist its encroachment if they so choose. For example, measures could be taken to improve the small farmer's ability to practice scientific farming of a sort adapted to his situation— that is, to small plots, with small-scale machinery. To do this would involve making available to him the advantages of a credit system, agricultural extension service, marketing and distribution system, suitable tools, irrigation, storage facilities, roads, and research facilities. For without economic and political protection, industrializaton leads to the demise of the small farm (as it did in the U.S.) and displacement of the farmer to the city (where he adds to urban problems). Similarly, mechanisms could be instituted to foster small-scale enterprises in manufacturing and commerce, instead of letting industrialization sweep away such "inefficient" operations.

The challenge to the world industrial system, then, is to reduce the barriers to modernization for those who choose that course, and simultaneously to increase the tolerance for diverse alternative societies so they too can participate in the world system while preserving their own cultural integrity. When a society chooses the path of industrial development, this tends to involve the conversion of the complete culture to an industrial mold; it requires a total revolution, involving all the social, cultural, and religious institutions; it alters attitudes, philosophy, and way of life. Some societies may not want to follow such a route.

The widening gap cannot be closed by changes in either the developing countries or the advanced countries alone. Resolution of the world distribution dilemma will not be achieved quickly or without anguish. Nor can it be achieved without vast changes in the world system— changes that involve the overall incentive structure of the world economy and profoundly affect the way of life in the rich countries as well as the poor. The change will require not only the comforting of the afflicted, but equally the afflicting of the comfortable.

The Hitler State by Magnus Zeller

CHAPTER SIX

THE CONTROL DILEMMA

PERHAPS THE ULTIMATE CHALLENGE facing man today can be summed up in a single question: Now that man has developed consummate skill in technology—the art of how to do things—can he develop equal ability to choose wisely which things are worth doing? This question places us face-to-face with a fourth dilemma. How can we exercise needed societal control over technology without sacrificing individual liberty?

Industrialized society now has, or could develop soon, the power:

1. To change to an unlimited degree the characteristics of our physical environment and the plant and animal population of the biosphere.

2. To modify without limit the physical characteristics of individual human bodies and the evolutionary development of the human race by means of biological and genetic engineering.

3. To alter drastically mankind's social and psychological environment, including people's mental and emotional characteristics.

4. To annihilate large segments of the human race and devastate large areas of the earth with weapons of mass destruction.

5. To change significantly, in many other ways, the kind of world that is handed to the next generation.

These powers are so awesome and vast that they clearly must be directed, channeled, and controlled. The citizenry is aware of the need for technological control. Battles over supersonic air transportation, pesticides, and air pollution, and the current clashes over the form and extent of nuclear power production are harbingers of more such controversies to come. The formation of the Office of Technology Assessment (1972) as an arm of Congress is indicative of the national awareness of the growing need for some mechanisms to guide new technology—to anticipate side effects, to assess future consequences, and to regulate technological development accordingly.

The dilemma regarding technological control arises because it is not clear whether more control can be exerted over new technology (e.g., who may develop and apply what technologies, with what future impacts on society) without seriously endangering fundamental features of private enterprise and our democratic society. Only a few years ago technological advancement seemed almost synonymous with "civilization." The history of science and technology was viewed as a continuum, with periods of acceleration and periods of stasis and now and then a great leap forward. Beginning with flint tools and the wheel and proceeding through metallurgy, the loom, and the steam engine, the great success story advanced to jet planes, satellites orbiting the earth, integrated circuits and pocket computers, and space flights putting man on the moon. And beyond these achievements, there were new wonders yet to come. Technological man seemed invincible.

Then, somewhat suddenly, in the last third of this century, the public became disenchanted with uncurbed technology; people demanded technological restraint and social responsibility. Whereas technological advance had formerly been considered an irresistible force, bringing with it unquestioned advantages and social progress, now a new alternative appeared possible—the rejection of some technologies because of their undesirable social impact. The new era was heralded by the 1971 Congressional decision to abandon development of the supersonic air transport. More broadly, the defeat of the SST signaled a new attitude toward all modern technology—an insistence that it must be subject to public decision in the political process.

It is not completely clear where crucial decisions about technology have been made in the past. One viewpoint is that no one was in charge —that technological change followed random discoveries and depended on market forces and the skills of particularly capable entrepreneurs.

Another view is that the centralized bureaucracies of governments and large corporations generated technology and controlled how it was used. Those who defend this latter view believe that technical decisions were made by a managerial elite and uncritically accepted as lying outside the decision-making capabilities of ordinary people; accordingly, technology is seen as a new source of power that has thus far been largely directed to the ends of established power groups.

In general, technological change has been widely accepted as an essential element of economic development. Economic growth depends upon gains in productivity that can be achieved only with the infusion of new knowledge and technology. In all sectors of human life, technology has enormously increased the range of opportunities for consumers, has opened up new horizons of communication and transportation, has brought greater life expectancy and relief from the sufferings of illness, and has contributed both comforts and pleasant diversions. Nevertheless, we now realize that the uncontrolled introduction of new technologies is not an unmitigated blessing. The growing awareness of the disruptive effect of technology has led not only to public dissatisfaction and disillusionment, but also to action.

The Art of Technology Assessment

In the future, the benefits and advantages of technology will be weighed against its costs and disadvantages. In other words, there will be a social accounting of technological change. This evaluation of costs and benefits will depend upon a new specialty called technology assessment. Technology assessment is the systematic analysis of the societal consequences of proposed technological change. It involves preparing a comprehensive description of the probable development of the technology under scrutiny, identifying all parties who potentially will be affected, investigating direct and indirect impacts in as broad and long-range fashion as possible, and preparing comparative evaluations of alternative technologies for accomplishing the same ends. Stated simply, technology assessment amounts to weighing carefully the full range of future costs and benefits involved in developing a proposed technology. The demand for technology assessment indicates a basic change in the public attitude toward science and technology; the public now insists on a better application of technology for the benefit of society as a whole.

By contrast, in the past, technology came under control only *after* its disadvantages became so obvious that public concern stimulated political pressure (e.g., the cases of strip mining, nuclear test fallout, DDT). Technology assessment attempts to provide earlier warning signals.

When technology assessment is instigated too late, the technology may be so well developed that it has already caused harm, or it may already represent such a massive investment that vested interests are entrenched and deeply committed to the technology's further development. In other words, the assessment failed to accomplish its mission. At the other extreme, suppose that the assessment is made long before the technology is fully developed. If the analysis shows that the probable social costs are greater than the expected benefits, should society step in and prohibit development of the technology in question? To do so implies a faith in the precision of analysis that is hardly justified. Moreover, opportunities for important learning and new discoveries might be missed. An argument is sometimes raised for developing the technology for the very purpose of assessing its social costs or for stimulating further discoveries. Furthermore, premature control would inhibit the freedom of the entrepreneur to a serious extent; it threatens to lead away from free enterprise and judgment by the marketplace and toward a centrally planned society. Dictatorship by technocrats may be as unwise and socially costly as living with the consequences of uncontrolled, rampant technology. Clearly, such a dictatorship is not a solution in keeping with the preservation of individual liberties. We must look further, for there is more to consider.

The decision whether to foster or prohibit a new technological development will never be easy. Technology nearly always affects some group's health, jobs, taxes, housing, education, or other vital concern. The groups and individuals thus affected are beginning to demand a right to some say in the decisions. Thus, the National Council for the Public Assessment of Technology has appeared. It is a nonprofit organization that informs citizen groups about new technologies and new applications of existing technologies, *before* they are implemented. Such citizen groups can be a positive force in helping us develop technologies that are socially desirable, environmentally benign, and economically creative. There is a danger, however, that our whole system of innovation could become paralyzed if it became necessary to secure approval from too many autonomous groups before a technological action could be taken.

Growing resistance to the idea of rampant technological development commandeering the future under the banner of progress leads us to realize that we need a technology assessment of technology itself. Technological growth takes on a life of its own, and man adapts to that. Such an assessment of technology would confront us even more squarely with the question of *how* technology is to be controlled. The attitudes that subtly infuse the culture are summarized in the quip that the ultimate solution to air pollution is the development of smog-resistant humans.

The premise, long built into the technological-industrial thrust, that any technology that *can* be developed and applied *should* be—the "technological imperative"—turns out to be pathogenic in the end. Like the sorcerer's apprentice, we do not know how to control the process when the consequences become intolerable.

An Example of Technology Assessment

For a concrete example of the difficulties involved in technology assessment, let us look at the need for the national utilization of coal. If the United States is to avoid intolerable costs for foreign petroleum, it must rapidly begin drawing on its Western coal reserves. Two of the major issues involved are the environmental impact of mining the coal and the level of production that should be set as a national target.

The technical alternatives are varied. Much of Western coal could be extracted by strip mining, but subsequent restoration of the land would be difficult because of scanty rainfall. The coal could be shipped to coal-burning plants in the East, it could be converted to electricity where it is mined, or it could be made into synthetic gaseous and liquid fuel. The environmental consequences would be different in each case. Water would be needed for mining, processing purposes, and land reclamation, but its use for such purposes would undoubtedly reduce the water available locally for present and future agricultural production. Large amounts of capital would be required, but might be provided by the federal government acting in the national interest. Such federal intervention, however, would imply a decision to have national interests override local concerns about the environmental impact on specific communities.

A key question at the national level involves production targets. How rapidly should exploitation be pushed? One point of view is that coal is required to bridge a gap between decreasing oil and gas production and ultimate massive dependence on controlled fusion power as the fundamental energy supply for an economy based on three "clean" intermediate energy forms—hydrogen, methanol, and electricity. Another view strongly espoused is that the possibility of primary dependence on clean, cheap fusion power before the oil and gas run out is an unfounded wishful dream. Rather, according to this argument, fossil fuels must supply our energy needs much longer; hence it is imperative to curb the exponential growth of energy use and reduce future energy demand.

If we accept the first premise, stimulating capital investment for coal is of highest priority. The second assumption, in contrast, assigns higher priority to answering the question: How can the whole society be restructured to reduce future energy demands markedly and yet not devastate the economy in the process? As we have argued previously, this latter course—restructuring society to reduce energy demands—would involve profound cultural changes in attitudes, buying patterns, lifestyles, work roles, operative values, and political behavior.

This interwoven set of energy, environmental, and economic issues is of the greatest importance to our future. These issues involve policy decisions that in the end will be made by, and certainly will affect, all of the American people. We need institutions to enable effective citizen participation in early stages of such technological control issues. These institutions need to be local, regional, national, and international. They need to form a highly effective interconnected network. Some of the components of the network would be governmental units at various levels; some would be in the private and nonprofit sectors; some would be in the voluntary sector (such as the National Council for Public Assessment of Technology, mentioned earlier). The important role that the voluntary sector could play has already been demonstrated by the environmentalist and consumer groups.

In general these institutions would have two tasks—to define and compare alternatives and to select and adopt the desired alternatives. The first task is technical, requiring advanced skills and detailed information. Facts are not politically neutral, and organization and interpretation of facts is certainly not neutral. Accordingly, although this work involves technical skills, citizens should not trustingly leave it in the hands of expert elites. The second task is political and even more clearly calls for citizen participation in stimulating needed action. The most effective organizational forms for accomplishing these two tasks have yet to emerge through experimentation. The basic principle is to obtain effective citizen participation in "designing the future" and to achieve necessary regulation at the lowest practicable level. These efforts may take place at the local community level for some issues, such as human welfare, and at the international level for others, such as oceanic pollution.

One aspect of the technical task is particularly urgent—the need to develop the means to equitably insert public costs (e.g., environmental impact, resource depletion, technological disemployment, overtaxing of public facilities) and benefits (e.g., aesthetic gain, conservation of nonrenewable resources, improved services) into the equations governing decisions on applications of new technology or introduction of new products, along with the private costs and benefits on which the decision is already presumably based.

This inclusion of public costs and benefits in the private decision-making process is the next step beyond technology assessment. Taxes on effluents to discourage pollution of air and water are an elementary example—the individual or firm is still free to pollute, but the tax influences his decision whether to or not. Such changes in the incentive system make it possible for the individual or the corporation to be socially responsible without paying an economic penalty. However, such incentives will be effective only to the extent that they are accepted and supported by the public.

At the international level, the large multinational corporations will have an important role to play in the planning process. The largest multinational corporations have more economic power than most nations, and national boundaries are especially permeable to them. More than most other social institutions, these corporations have a vested interest in the future well-being of the world economy. They have the technical and financial resources and also the potential motivation to contribute to better planning for habitability of the entire planet.

In the end the legitimating and de-legitimating power of the world citizenry (acting perhaps through supranational agencies set up by the United Nations or through voluntary associations) is the most persuasive inducement to the large corporations to be responsible citizens of the world.

Planning has been attempted before, of course—for determining land use, curbing pollution, easing disemployment stemming from technological changes, improving urban transportation, and controlling the environmental impact of industrial activity. To date, such planning has been extremely limited in effectiveness, partly because sufficient moral force was not exerted on behalf of social needs, and partly because economic incentives often operated counter to socially desirable actions.

Citizen-participation planning could be more effective now and in the future for several reasons. There is greater public interest in planning for the future, new tools exist for redesigning incentive systems to support socially responsible behavior, and cultural pressures are mounting against irresponsible institutions. Thus, there is at least some hope that we can learn to control our new Faustian powers over our physical and social environment.

Social Change in a Democracy

How do societies change? Some of the issues involved in technology control will become clearer if we consider a simple model that addresses this question. In the course of their activities the various elements of society—individuals, groups, corporations, and government agencies—make what we may term *microdecisions* (e.g., to buy a certain product, to employ a person for a particular task, to develop and market a new product, to enact a piece of legislation). These microdecisions interact and lead to *macrodecisions* affecting the overall society (e.g., price and wage levels, a 4 percent annual growth rate in energy usage, a 10 percent inflation rate, deterioration of the central cities, pollution of the environment, depletion of nonrenewable resources). The basic problem is that *perfectly reasonable microdecisions, by all the criteria that have governed in the past, are currently adding up to largely unsatisfactory macrodecisions*. This constitutes the fundamental management dilemma of industrialized society. To recognize this is to stop searching for someone to blame, and to start searching for the sorts of changes that would make the process start working again.

Adam Smith, in *The Wealth of Nations,* justified capitalism by claiming that when the entrepreneur "intends only his own gain . . . he is . . . led by an invisible hand to promote an end which was no part of his intention. . . . By pursuing his own interest he frequently promotes that of the society more effectually than when he really intends to promote it." By now we know the reverse may frequently also be true because individuals often choose on the basis of their own short-term, imprudent self-interest instead of long-term, enlightened self-interest. Accordingly, the invisible hand clearly needs a little help. Such help has existed for years in the form of government control via antitrust laws, commerce regulations, Keynesian manipulations of the money supply and interest rates, and so on. Yet the basic management dilemma worsens.

The fundamental problem is not simply a matter of tradeoffs—it is that the tradeoffs seem to grow steadily more intolerable. As one cartoon caption described it, "There's a pricetag on everything. You want a high standard of living, you settle for a low quality of life."

An obvious solution would be to select desired macrodecisions and derive microdecisions from them. The logic is appealing. It would seem possible to select appropriate national and planetary goals that are in accord with the best available knowledge regarding human fulfillment, and then determine what types of microdecisions would be necessary to achieve those goals.

But there is a catch. The *means* used to obtain those necessary individual actions have to be compatible with the ends. In a democratic society one cannot dictate goals—even desirable ones. There is no set of paramount objectives that, once chosen, unambiguously guides the actions of society. Rather, there are sets of goals, often mutually inconsistent or partially conflicting (e.g., local decision making, energy self-sufficiency, environmental protection, economic growth, positive incentives where possible, private sector actions preferred to public sector actions where feasible). The macrodecision delineating the priority to be attached to each goal varies with time and is simply a matter of what wins out in the political process; there is no timeless set of priorities. The microdecisions necessary to actualize the chosen goals have to be guided primarily by an understanding of the linkages among them. Forcing correct microdecisions by coercive decrees or behavior manipulation is obviously incompatible with basic democratic principles.

Thus we begin to see what kind of technology management is compatible with the basic character of a democratic society. The example of environmental protection will help clarify the issue. Changing public awareness during the decade of the 1960s resulted in the macrodecision to place a somewhat higher priority than before on the preservation and enhancement of the physical environment; one consequence of this macrodecision was the National Environmental Protection Act of 1970. Subsequent developments made it clear that environmental protection is not as simple as setting and enforcing clean air and water standards. Environmental deterioration is directly related to the rate of use of energy and resources, and that in turn to economic growth. The decision to preserve and enhance the environment implies decisions to pay higher prices for products to cover costs of environmental protection and probably, in the longer run, decisions to evolve toward a more frugal kind of civilization, which may involve changes in consumer patterns and life-styles, industrial processes and products, agricultural methods and the rural way of life, population distribution, and social goals. All aspects of individual life will eventually be affected. For all this to take place—for the macrodecision to preserve and enhance the environment to in fact be made by the society—requires a collective and voluntary redirection of the whole society, with widespread understanding of the implications of the macrodecision and willingness to make individual microdecisions in accord with the overall social choice. It also requires institutional changes for effectively employing widespread citizen participation at local, regional, national, and global levels. In sum, the key decisions are made at the macrodecision level. These involve long-term goals and must be made in the democratic political process, with citizen involvement from the start. Successful implementation of a new macrodecision calls for reeducation of the whole society so that people understand the implications of the macrodecision and can make their own individual microdecisions in accord with the overall policy. Nothing less than this sort of cultural and institutional change will resolve the dilemma of achieving adequate management of technology without sacrificing liberty.

The Ancient of Days by William Blake

CHAPTER SEVEN

THE CHANGING IMAGE OF MAN

THE APPARENT INABILITY of the industrial-era paradigm to resolve the fundamental dilemmas of technologically advanced society has caused many contemporary observers to ask whether more adequate guiding patterns can be found. At the same time, the seemingly spontaneous appearance of a new transcendentalism has brought renewed concern with the fundamental moral and value premises that shape every society. The old paradigm brought with it a growth-and-consumption ethic that has proven inadequate to provide political guidance and to command the deepest loyalties of society's citizens; its prediction-and-control oriented, technology-aimed science has debunked the sorts of transcendental values that have guided Western civilization in its noblest moments. Just as industrial society is pushed toward a new dominant paradigm by the four dilemmas we have examined, it is pulled toward that development by a newly emerging image of man, which promises to restore paramountcy to the quest for human growth in a humane society.

A principal feature of the industrial paradigm has been the concept that man is activated largely by economic motivations. Whether an individual is concerned with a real need for food and shelter or a perceived need for a vacation in the country, his economic behavior and the functioning of the economic system are assumed to be fairly dependable and predictable—so much so that a science of economics has been erected positing that man's economic behavior and his functioning in the economic system are both predictable and modelable, much as is the behavior of molecules in a gas. We tend to forget that this dominating and institution-honored concern with economic motivation could turn out to be quite transient and parochial. Other societies and social groupings have placed more emphasis on other motivations—the social forces of tradition, identification with the common welfare, tribal loyalty, patriotism, moral righteousness, or the search for enlightenment.

Alternative Images of Man

But it would be too simple to say that economic considerations are the only factors influencing individuals in our society. Here are five more fundamental images of man, which have coexisted to some extent with the economic image in recent decades:

1. *Man as a physiologically motivated mechanism*, responding to stimuli in his environment as they impinge upon his physical sense organs.

2. *Man as a psychologically conditioned animal*, with instinctive energies and desires modulated by social conditioning acting through such subconscious processes as repression, resistance, sublimation, etc.

3. *Man as a free being*, possessing the capacity to exercise free choice with self-awareness of his existential condition, endowed with reason, intentionality, and a valid sense of value.

4. *Man as God's creation*, possessing both human freedom and the moral responsibility to act according to God's will as perceived through revelation.

5. *Man as a transcendental being*, who has "the Divine within," a "true Self" or "Atman" or "Oversoul," which the individual may come to experience as one with a "Higher Spirit," "Brahman," or the "Divine Ground."

Human society is not yet past battling over which of these or other images describes the "true" nature of man. Nonetheless we are becoming increasingly aware that reality is simply too rich to be expressed fully in any one image or metaphor. Just as physicists learned the folly of fighting over whether light is composed of waves or particles, and came to see these as complementary metaphors, so we are gradually coming to realize that such well-worn dichotomies as free will versus determinism, physical versus spiritual, and science versus religion are really only expressions of the tension between complementary and equally valid metaphors.

Still, to whatever extent one such image of man can be said to be dominant in our culture, it is a valid and important question whether that dominant image of man seems to be changing. For surely if it is, that will affect all aspects of the social culture.

Of all society's institutions, education is most directly and fundamentally based on an image of man's basic nature, his process of development, and his ultimate relationship to the universe around him. Obviously the findings of scientific research influence society's image of man, but so also does the prevailing image of man shape the choice of scientific inquiries and the way they are carried out. The concepts of democracy and free enterprise, legal and governmental structures and processes, the definitions of criminality and how it is dealt with, treatment of the poor and the handicapped—all stem from our underlying image of man.

Challenges to Scientific Orthodoxy

All societies have their official or recognized truth-seeking activities and institutions. In the Western world science holds this position as the official arbiter of truth. As with other societies and other ways of discerning and validating truth, we have been taught that our way is best. What comes to be accepted in the scientific community as truth has significant consequences for the basic beliefs of our culture. Hence it is both interesting and important to glance back over the past century and a half of scientific history to observe how this acceptance has come about.

One of the oldest areas of psychological knowledge has to do with those strange phenomena grouped together under the term *hypnosis*. Hypnotism has been studied systematically for more than a century and a half, although its admittance to scientific respectability is much more recent. Among the scientifically demonstrated aspects of hypnosis are that hypnotic suggestion can bring about local or general loss of sensation (anesthesia) and the absence of a sense of pain (analgesia); positive and negative hallucinations; regression to an earlier age; unusual muscular strength, rigidity, and resistance to fatigue; and bodily changes normally outside voluntary control.

The anesthetic and analgesic potentialities of hypnosis were demonstrated a century ago in hundreds of apparently painless major operations, some witnessed by scores of physicians. Yet the possibility of the phenomenon's existence was denied, and medical journals refused to publish papers documenting the work. Patients were accused of deluding or conspiring with their doctors by pretending to feel no pain while limbs were cut off or abdominal operations were performed.

Hypnosis has experienced a long history of irrational opposition. It is not clear just why presumably rational observers rejected these phenomena so vigorously. Perhaps it is because they challenge our very concept of reality by raising doubts about our ability to know or judge what is real. But the important point here is that scientists once felt very uncomfortable with hypnosis, and now feel quite comfortable— despite the fact that the basic mechanism cannot be "explained" any better now than before. The phenomena remain mysterious, but the mystery has ceased to disturb us.

The concept of unconscious processes, too, became acceptable to scientists only recently. The initial reaction to the hypotheses of Freud and other pioneers in this area was one of disturbance and hostility, rationalized in a number of ingenious ways. To be sure, these are strange ideas: the concept that there are mental processes over which we exert no control and of which we have only sporadic or inferred knowledge; that we repress information, distorting or hiding it from our conscious awareness and lying to ourselves; that one level of our psyche deceives or sends cryptic messages to another part. But, over time, the strange became familiar, the uncomfortable became comfortable, and unconscious processes became a useful and accepted psychological concept.

The initial reaction was similarly hostile to the concepts of psychosomatic illness and the power of self-suggestion—the idea that mentally we may cause our own bodily ailments, unconsciously contribute to our "accident proneness," or self-suggest our successes and failures. The disquieting implication was that we have, in some unconscious sense, far deeper power over and understanding of the functioning of our total organisms than our conscious mind ordinarily admits.

When F.W.H. Myers' *Human Personality* was published in 1903, summarizing preliminary explorations into taboo areas of extraordinary psychic phenomena, it included in this category not only unconscious processes and hypnosis but also sleep and dreams and creativity (which Myers called "inspiration"). The virtually universal testimony of highly creative individuals has been that their created projects are the result of higher, unconscious processes over which they have only limited control. Myers' vanguard parapsychological treatise stressed the essential similarities between such psychic phenomena as telepathy and clairvoyance and the experiences of creative geniuses and of mathematical prodigies. Three-quarters of a century ago creativity was part of the domain of psychic research and was hardly scientifically respectable.

During the past quarter century the new tools of biofeedback and related explorations have provided startling revelations. Inner mental states have been shown to have physically measurable correlates—rapid eye movements, changes in skin resistance, muscle tensions, electro-encephalogram (brain-wave) components, and electric and magnetic fields around the body. Furthermore, when these indicators are picked up by sensors and returned to the brain as feedback signals (e.g., as light, sound, or meter readings), all sorts of involuntary bodily processes and states can be brought under voluntary control. Provided feedback from temperature sensors on the fingertips, the individual discovers that he can control the blood flow and hence temperature in his extremities. Feedback from muscle-tension sensors leads to the ability to relieve headaches and spasms. Indications of brain-wave activity allow the individual to control passage into different mental states. In these phenomena investigators found not only a whole new kit of tools, but also a new basis for legitimating studies of man's inner world of experience. Because scientists feel more secure when they can observe pointer readings, they could now accept studying such experience.

Again the implications are profound. Apparently we know, at some unconscious level, how to control the circulation in our fingertips; however, because of the absence of suitable feedback, this control ordinarily goes on totally outside our realm of conscious awareness. In a similar sense we also know how we grow our hair, assimilate our food, and heal bodily injuries; the processes are ordinarily involuntary and out of conscious awareness, but *under certain conditions voluntary control may be assumed and even some sort of conscious understanding of the process may be experienced*. Scientists and laymen alike have found the implications of such findings difficult to assimilate, but again, given time, they are becoming comfortable with them.

There are presently two important areas of research about which the majority of scientists still feel some discomfort—discomfort which we may assume will also diminish with time. One of these areas deals with the beginning of a systematic study of various states of consciousness—including familiar states from deep sleep to creative awareness—with particular attention to those inner experiences that have formed the bases for the world's religions and out of which have come man's deepest value commitments. The other area covers the important testing ground of psychic research.

The Discordant Data of Psychic Research

This second area is important precisely because it lies midway between and links together the objective world of public observation, which is the domain of "ordinary" science, and the private world of subjective experience, heretofore a realm left to the humanities and religion. Psychic phenomena are anomalous—their occurrence is widely attested to, yet they do not conform to known physical and biological laws. They do suggest, however, that something is fundamentally incomplete about a world view which cannot accommodate their existence. They also serve as a sort of reality test for the universe of inner experience. Such experiences are not wholly "inner"—they include something publicly observable. Neither are they wholly "outer," since some activity of the subjective mind is clearly involved.

The following list will serve to stake out the territory of psychic phenomena under discussion:

- *Telepathy*, the apparently extrasensory communication by one mind to another.
- *Clairvoyance*, the apparently extrasensory perception of aspects of the physical world, including clairvoyant diagnosis of illness, clairvoyant "seeing" events at a remote location, and clairvoyant perception of information about a past owner or user of a physical object.
- *Faith healing*, healing more rapid than, or beyond, that which can be accounted for by known organic processes.
- *Retrocognition*, the "remembering" of events that happened to some other person, or prior to the birth of the "rememberer."
- *Precognition*, the "remembering" of events sometime in the future.
- *Psychokinesis*, the apparent influencing of the physical world through mental processes (e.g., levitation, teleportation) rather than physical processes.
- *Unusual control of involuntary processes* (e.g., stigmata, fire-walking).
- *Thought photography*, the production of an image on a photographic film apparently through mental processes alone.
- *Unusual mental abilities* (e.g., speaking in unknown tongues, mathematical prodigies).

Evidence mounts that these sorts of preternormal knowings and abilities are latent in all persons but are typically highly repressed. For example, one experiment that points in this direction depends upon the discovery that a stroboscopic light flashing in the eyes, when the frequency of flashes is somewhere near the natural alpha frequency of the brain (around 10 cycles per second), can induce a distinctive component in the brain-wave pattern. In the experiment two remotely isolated persons participate. The stroboscopic light is flashed in one person's eyes, and the brain wave of the second person is monitored. The second person is typically unable to guess any better than he could by chance whether or not the stimulus is being applied to the first person during a given time interval. Nevertheless, the second person's subliminal response in his brain wave indicates that unconsciously he knows. (A necessary condition for successful extrasensory communication in this experiment seems to be that the two persons have some rapport and that one is paying attention to the other—but we have no more adequate explanation for what it means to "pay attention" than we do for extrasensory perception.) If we extrapolate beyond this particular situation, the implication of such an experiment is that we may eventually discover that we all possess a full range of psychic potentialities, which are generally almost completely repressed.

It is important to understand both why these two research areas of consciousness exploration and psychic phenomena have so disturbed scientists in the past and also why the reconciliation now seems close at hand. The extent of the potential impact of these two areas on the scientific world view is suggested by the following list of premises that the scientific paradigm, until recently, has tended to imply:

1. The only way man acquires knowledge is through his physical senses and perhaps through some sort of memory storage in the genes.

2. All qualitative properties are ultimately reducible to quantitative ones; in other words, color can be reduced to wavelength, hate and love to the chemical composition of glandular secretions, etc.

3. There is a clear distinction between the objective world, which is perceivable by anyone, and subjective experience, which is perceived by the individual alone in the privacy of his own mind.

4. The concept of "the free inner person" is a prescientific explanation for behavior, whereas behavior is really determined by forces impinging upon the individual from his environment and interacting with internal tensions and pressures that are characteristic of the organism. From the influential standpoint of behavioral science, psychic freedom and free choice are mere illusions. "Freedom" is behavior for which scientists have not yet found the cause.

5. What we know as consciousness, or awareness of our thoughts and feelings, is really only a side effect of physical and biochemical processes going on in the brain.

6. What we know as memory is simply a matter of stored data in the physical organism, strictly comparable with the storage of information in a digital computer. Thus it is impossible for a person to "remember" an event that happened to someone else in a different lifetime.

7. Given the nature of time, there is obviously no way we can obtain advance knowledge of the future other than by rational prediction from known causes. Thus it is impossible for anyone to "remember" an event happening sometime in the future.

8. Since mental activity is simply a matter of fluctuating states in the physical organism, it is completely impossible for a person's mental activity to exert any direct effect on the physical world outside the organism, other than through the normal functioning of his psychomotor system.

9. The evolution of man and the universe has come about through purely physical causes, through random mutations and natural selection. There is no justification, either in the evolution of consciousness or in the strivings of individuals, for any belief in universal purpose or a goal-directed evolutionary urge.

10. The individual does not survive the death of the organism; or if there is any sense in which the individual exists after the death of his physical body, we can neither comprehend it in this life nor in any way obtain knowledge about it.

Research into consciousness and psychic phenomena is such a bitterly contested battleground because the data in these areas challenge *all* of the above premises. Yet it was on the basis of these premises that the increasingly prestigious scientific world view was able, in the past, to dismiss as of secondary consequence the religious, aesthetic, and intuitive experiences of man and hence to discredit value systems based in those subjective experiences.

The Ultimate Question of Consciousness

These two interrelated research areas (consciousness exploration and psychic phenomena) seem to threaten the concepts of modern science because they so evidently involve the ultimate question: How do I know what I know, and how do I know it is "true"? In *Wind, Sand, and Stars* Antoine de Saint-Exupéry provided a basic definition of truth: "Truth is *not* that which is demonstrable. Truth is that which is ineluctable"— that which cannot be escaped.

How do I know what is ineluctable? This question is at the heart of the discipline of epistemology, the study of the nature of human knowledge. Essentially there are two quite different forms of knowing, and we all use both daily. One form is *knowing about things in the manner of scientific facts*; it is based in rational, empirical processes. The other form is *knowing by intuitive identification with*, as in knowing another person; it is based to considerable extent in unconscious processes. Modern writers are fond of associating these two forms of knowing with the left and right sides of the brain.

The second kind of knowing is what the poet Archibald MacLeish refers to when he wrote, "We *really* know a thing only when we are filled with a wonderfully full, new, and intimate sense of it and, above all, of our relation with it. This sense—this *knowledge*—art can give but abstraction [science] cannot." The Indian scholar Radhakrishnan, describing perception in the higher stages of consciousness, explains, "The conscious division and separation of . . . the object from the subject, which is the normal condition, is broken down. The individual surrenders to the object and is absorbed by it. He becomes what he beholds." Robert Browning insists in the poem "Paracelsus" that in the end this second knowing is supreme:

> Truth is within ourselves; it takes no rise
> From outward things, whate'er you may believe.
> There is an inmost center in us all
> Where truth abides in fullness; and around,
> Wall upon wall, the gross flesh hems it in,
> This perfect, clear perception—which is truth.
> A baffling and perverting carnal mesh
> Binds it, and makes all error: and to know,
> Rather consists in opening out a way
> Whence the imprisoned splendour may escape,
> Than in effecting entry for a light
> Supposed to be without.

Both kinds of knowledge are subject to the possibility of error. The scientific way of "knowing about" involves meticulous testing to insure that what is claimed as fact can be validated by other scientists making similar experiments or explorations. But "intuitive knowing" also demands careful testing to prevent self-deception. The astonishing extent to which our mental processes can be altered by unconscious factors must lead us to doubt how well we know even that most intimate being, our own self. (At best I seem to reveal to my conscious self only a small and badly distorted fragment of the wholeness that is "me.") Even so, it is not futile to seek self-knowledge; from each new vantage point we seem to be able to look back and observe how we have fooled ourselves in a previous and lower state of awareness.

Thus, in opening up the exploration of consciousness, scientists are forced to confront questions that, throughout most of the history of scientific activity, they have managed to set aside for the philosophers to puzzle over. What are the essential limitations of "knowledge about," or factual knowledge? What are the ultimate capabilities of the mind as an observing instrument in discerning intuitive knowledge of the universe and of the mind itself? What are the ways in which intuitive knowledge is best shared and validated? In some sense *all* knowledge is ultimately subjective, since the root of all experience is consciousness. Consequently, these new explorations that probe the nature of consciousness are fundamental indeed; this probing of the nature of consciousness is where science, religion, and philosophy meet. We can hardly blame the scientists if their resolution quavers at this point and their anxieties become more evident than usual.

The types of papers currently being presented at scientific meetings and articles being published in the most prestigious scientific journals suggest that, with regard to both consciousness research and psychic research, the transition from rejection to acceptance may be at hand. This change can be partially attributed to the recent findings previously discussed—that there are physical and physiological correlates to inner experience. These findings serve to legitimate the inquiry into consciousness. More importantly, the change is a response to the growing awareness among scientists that "science" does not deal with reality in some ultimate sense, but with models and metaphors. This realization has brought about a change in attitude and a more promising climate for exploration of inner experience than heretofore.

A precursor to this realization came in the early part of this century with the resolution of the battle in physics, referred to earlier, over the nature of light—whether light is composed of waves or particles. The fighting ended when proponents of both views recognized that "wave" and "particle" are only models or metaphors that express certain aspects of the transcendental nature of light. (So, too, is the quantum mechanical equation that expresses quantitatively the relationship between the two aspects.) Certain photoelectric effects have no explanation in terms of

O *Waste of Loss* by Hans Erni

the wave image of light. On the other hand, the electron microscope is unexplainable with a mechanical particle model of electrons, but can be understood using a wave image. The resolution of this issue set a pattern for the resolution of others.

Thus the argument that attempted to resolve whether man is directed by free will *or* scientific determinism becomes instead a recognition that alternative metaphors are valid in expressing different aspects of a transcendental reality. In a similar way, the old-fashioned warfare between science and religion is rapidly dissolving because of the recognition that conventional scientific knowledge is essentially a set of metaphors useful for expressing certain aspects of ordinary, physical experience. Other aspects, especially man's deeper inner experience, demand other kinds of metaphors. We have yet to discover what particular metaphors will be most useful for our time; those that had the power to move men's hearts in the past seem less useful now.

A New Image of Man: The Perennial Philosophy

Even though these scientific developments on the frontier of consciousness have not progressed very far, it is possible to infer in which direction they will push our image of man and his place in the universe. Wherever the nature of man has been probed deeply, in Eastern or Western traditions, the paramount fact that emerges is the duality of his experience. He is found to be both physical and spiritual, both aspects being "real" and neither fully describable in terms of the other. Hence scientific and religious metaphors are complementary; neither contradicts the other. Both are required to deal with man's wholeness.

If this new exploration of human nature is in part a *rediscovery*, that does not mean the change would be simply a return to a cultural wholeness we once knew; it would be advancing to a new evolutionary stage of awareness that has no real counterpart in history. As P.W. Martin, author of *Experiment in Depth*, explains:

> It is evident that, throughout the ages, individuals and communities have repeatedly come upon the creative factors and forces at work in the human psyche. Great philosophies and great religions have time and time again come into being as an outcome of such discoveries, and for a while stirred men to the depths. But as often as the discoveries have been made they have again been lost. In this present age there is the possibility of making the discoveries in a new way. . . . For the first time in history, the scientific spirit of inquiry, the free search for truth, is being turned upon the other side of consciousness.

In place of *a priori* dogma there is a growing body of empirically established experience; experience which can be progressively funded, as our experience of the outer world has been funded, and its meaning learned. Because of this, there is good prospect that the discoveries can this time be held and so become, now and henceforward, no longer the lost secret but the living heritage of man.

The image of man and the concept of the ultimate nature of knowledge and reality that can be expected to emerge, then, is not entirely new. There is an identifiable view of man-in-the-universe that Aldous Huxley calls "the perennial philosophy" in his book of the same name. According to Huxley, the perennial philosophy is "immemorial and universal." He explains:

> Rudiments of the Perennial Philosophy may be found among the traditionary lore of primitive peoples in every region of the world, and in its fully developed forms it has a place in every one of the higher religions. A version of this Highest Common Factor in all preceding and subsequent theologies was first committed to writing more than twenty-five centuries ago, and since that time the inexhaustible theme has been treated again and again, from the standpoint of every religious tradition and in all the principal languages of Asia and Europe.

In its Western form, the ethic deriving from the perennial philosophy comprises an intermittently visible stream and has had a profound effect on Western civilization. Thales, Solon, Pythagoras, and Plato journeyed to Egypt to be initiated into the ancient Mysteries. Much of the perennial philosophy is woven into the structure of Christianity. In its Hermetic, Cabbalistic, Sufistic, Rosicrucian, and Freemasonry forms it greatly influenced the history of the Middle East, Europe, and the United States.

We propose to summarize the main characteristics of this perennial philosophy here and in the next chapter to examine what it would mean *if* this view of man-in-the-universe were to become dominant.

Essential Characteristics of the Perennial Philosophy

The first important thing to be noted about the perennial philosophy is that its adherents have always insisted that it is *not* a philosophy or a metaphysic, *not* an ideology or a religious belief. (Nevertheless, others have typically considered it so.) Huxley, for example, describes it as "the thing—the metaphysic that recognizes a divine Reality substantial to the world of things and lives and minds; the psychology that finds in the soul something similar to, or even identical with, divine Reality; the ethic that places man's final end in the knowledge of the imminent and transcendent Ground of all being."

The flavor of the perennial philosophy can perhaps best be conveyed by a selection of brief quotations from writers and sages of all ages. For convenience they are grouped into five categories: being, awareness, motivation, potentiality, and attitude.

Being. Central to the perennial philosophy is the proposition that man can under certain conditions attain a higher awareness, a "cosmic consciousness," in which he has immediate knowledge of a reality underlying the physical world. In speaking of this state it seems appropriate to use such words as infinite and eternal. From this vantage point, one's own growth and creativity, and one's participation in the evolutionary process, are seen to be under the ultimate direction of a higher center.

> The *atma*, the Self, is never born and never dies. It is without a cause and is eternally changeless. It is beyond time, unborn, permanent, and eternal. It does not die when the body dies. Concealed in the heart of all beings lies the *atma*, the Spirit, the Self; smaller than the smallest atom, greater than the greatest spaces (*Upanishads*, 1000 B.C.).
>
> Behold but One in all things (Kabir).
>
> Of all the hard facts of science, I know of none more solid and fundamental than the fact that if you inhibit thought (and persevere) you come at length to a region of consciousness below or behind thought and different from ordinary thought in its nature and character—a consciousness of quasi-universal quality, and a realization of an altogether vaster self than that to which we are accustomed. And since the ordinary consciousness, with which we are concerned in ordinary life, is before all things founded on the little, local self, it follows that to pass out of that is to die to the ordinary self and the ordinary world.
>
> It is to die in the ordinary sense, but in another sense it is to wake up and find that the I, one's real, most intimate self, pervades the universe and all other beings—that the mountains and the sea and the stars are a part of one's body and that one's soul is in touch with the souls of all creatures. It is to be assured of an indestructible immortal life and of a joy immense and inexpressible (Edward Carpenter, *Towards Democracy*).

Awareness. According to the perennial philosophy, man goes through life in a sort of hypnotic sleep, feeling that he is making decisions, having accidents happen to him, meeting chance acquaintances, and so on. If he begins to see more clearly, he becomes aware of the direction of the higher Self in this process. He becomes aware that decisions, which he felt he had come to logically or through intuition, were instead reflections of choices made on the higher level of the Self; that experiences and relationships which he needed for his growth were attracted to him by the Self and were by no means as accidental as they seemed at the time. What we know as inspiration or creativity is essentially a breaking through of these higher processes, "as if a fountain of Mind were welling up, bubbling to expression within prepared spirits" (Thomas Kelly). "When it breathes through his intellect, it is genius; when it breathes through his will, it is virtue; when it flows through his affection, it is love" (Ralph Waldo Emerson, "The Oversoul").

> Humanity is asleep, concerned only with what is useless, living in a wrong world (Sanai of Afghanistan, A.D. 1130).
>
> If the doors of perception were cleansed, everything would appear to man as it is, infinite.
> For man has closed himself up, 'til he sees all things thro' narrow chinks in his cavern (William Blake, *Marriage of Heaven and Hell*).
>
> In the ordinary state man is hypnotized and this hypnotic state is continually maintained and strengthened in him. . . . "To awaken" for man means to be "dehypnotized" (P.D. Ouspensky, *In Search of the Miraculous*).

Because ordinary perception is experienced as a *partial* perception, the language built up from it proves inadequate to describe the greater reality. Or, as Lao-Tse said in 550 B.C., "True words always seem paradoxical but no other form of teaching can take their place."

> Having realized his own self as the Self, a man becomes selfless; and in virtue of selflessness he is to be conceived as unconditioned. This is the highest mystery, betokening emancipation (*Upanishads*).
>
> Whoever seeks to gain his life will lose it; but whoever loses his life will preserve it (Jesus of Nazareth).
>
> The more we understand the whole of Being, the more we can tolerate the simultaneous existence and perception of inconsistencies, of oppositions and of flat contradictions. These seem to be products of partial cognition, and fade away with

cognition of the whole (Abraham Maslow, *Toward a Psychology of Being*).

In all the foregoing passages, the fundamental phenomenon is man hiding from himself. Accordingly, becoming aware—awakening, becoming dehypnotized—is a process of overcoming defenses, of realizing that which is already there.

> Oh, let the self exalt itself, not sink itself below: Self is the only friend of self, and self Self's only foe. For self, when it subdues itself, befriends itself. And so when it eludes self-conquest, is its own and only foe (*Bhagavad-Gita*).

> We tend to be afraid of any knowledge that could cause us to despise ourselves or make us feel inferior, weak, worthless, evil, shameful. We protect ourselves and our ideal image of ourselves by repression and similar defenses. . . . But there is another kind of truth we tend to evade. Not only do we hang on to our psychopathology, but also we tend to evade personal growth because this, too, can bring another kind of fear, of awe, of feelings of weakness and inadequacy. And so we find another kind of resistance, a denying of our best side, of our talents, of our finest impulse, of our highest potentialities, of our creativeness. . . . It is precisely the god-like in ourselves that we are ambivalent about, fascinated by and fearful of, motivated to and defensive against (Abraham Maslow, *Toward a Psychology of Being*).

Motivation. According to the perennial philosophy, when man comes to know himself, the pull of his material and ego needs is greatly lessened and he finds that his deepest motivation is to participate fully, with awareness, in the evolutionary process. Evolution is seen to be not a random matter, but directed by a higher consciousness and characterized by purpose. This purpose includes the development of individual centers of consciousness with freedom of choice, gradually moving toward ever-increasing knowledge of themselves, of Self, and of the Whole. Knowledge of and participation in this evolution is the supreme value. Gerald Heard summarized this view when he wrote, in *The Third Morality*, "Life does not need comfort, when it can be offered meaning, nor pleasure, when it can be shown purpose. Reveal what is the purpose and how he may attain it—the steps he must take—and man will go forward again hardily, happily, knowing that he has found what he must have—intentional living."

This quest for unitive understanding has sometimes seemed to Westerners to connote quietistic retreat. However, history displays some quite activist forms of the perennial philosophy, including the Sufistic form in the Islamic empire and the Rosicrucian-Freemasonry forms in the history of Western civilization.

Potentiality. Another tenet of the perennial philosophy is that human potentiality is limitless, that all knowledge and power is ultimately accessible to the mind looking within itself, and that all limitations are ultimately self-chosen. Such supranormal phenomena as telepathic communication, clairvoyant perception, retrocognition, clairvoyant diagnosis, faith healing, precognition, and psychokinesis are in general perfectly possible. At some deep level the individual understands these phenomena, and at some deep level he chooses the ordinary "physical laws" that on the whole preclude such psychic phenomena.

> Man is made by his belief. . . . As he believes, so he is (*Bhagavad-Gita*).

> I have no doubt whatever that most people live, whether physically, intellectually or morally, in a very restricted circle of their potential being. They make use of a very small portion of their possible consciousness, and of the soul's resources in general, much like a man who, out of his whole bodily organism, should get into a habit of using and moving only his little finger. . . . We all have reservoirs of life to draw upon, of which we do not dream (William James, 1906, quoted in Gardner Murphy, ed., *William James on Psychical Research*).

Attitude. Awareness leads to a new attitude toward life. We have noted previously that one aspect of this new attitude is the desire to participate consciously, to labor and serve, in the evolutionary process, the fulfillment of mankind. But the reverse side of this attitude is *acceptance*, the choosing of what *is*, since at some deep level the self already chooses this.

> To those who ask "What shall I do" we have finally one simple answer: "Accept yourself." To those who ask "But when I have accepted myself, what then?" we answer, "By your question you show that you have read without comprehension." To those who demur: "But you say nothing of man's duties— the world problems—peace or war—social reform—morality" we reply, "No, we say nothing of these things." His attitude to these things each man must let his accepted self determine. . . . What values a man will perpetuate, what values he can perpetuate, it is for himself to decide. We claim no more

than perhaps to help him to a condition where these questions decide themselves with a different and higher authority than any imposed decisions of the unintegrated self could ever possess (John Middleton Murry, *God*).

It is of capital importance to understand this distinction between acceptance and resignation. To accept, really to accept a situation, is to think and feel with the whole of one's being that, even if one had the faculty of modifying it, one would not do it, and would have no reason to do it (Hubert Benoit, *The Supreme Doctrine*).

We cannot change anything unless we accept it. . . . I do not in the least mean that we must never pass judgment. . . . But if the doctor wishes to help a human being he must be able to accept him as he is. And he can do this in reality only when he has already seen and accepted himself as he is. . . . Perhaps this sounds very simple, but simple things are always the most difficult (C.G. Jung).

Another important and related aspect is *nonattachment*—being "divinely impersonal," unbound to specific outcomes.

Therefore, do thou ever perform without attachment the work that thou must do; for performing action without attachment man attains the Supreme (*Bhagavad-Gita*).

A corollary of nonattachment is *impersonal love*, the most difficult to delineate because the coinage has been so debased in all that has been written about other emotions that also go by the name of love.

Love, which is the deification of persons, must become more impersonal every day . . . a love which knows not sex, nor person, nor partiality. . . . There are moments when the affections rule and absorb the man and make his happiness dependent on a person or persons. But in health the mind is presently seen again, its over-arching vault bright with galaxies of immutable lights, and the warm loves and fears, that swept over us as clouds, must lose their finite character and blend with God, to attain their own perfection (Ralph Waldo Emerson, "Essay on Love").

I have to know the other person and myself objectively in order to be able to see his reality, or rather, to overcome the illusions, the irrationally distorted picture I have of him. Only if I know a human being objectively, can I know him in his ultimate essence, in the act of love (Erich Fromm, *The Art of Loving*).

For thousands of years, then, men of different races and creeds have rediscovered the fundamental human experience revealed in the perennial philosophy. Continuity is one of the fundamental characteristics of human societies. Perhaps it should occasion no surprise that the basic elements of a world view which has moved mankind so powerfully in the past should take on new vigor again as the inherent dilemmas of the industrial-era paradigm become more and more apparent.

A New Freemasonry?

Despite the long history of the perennial philosophy, one might still seriously question whether it would ever be actively adopted by pragmatic Americans who have been so strongly motivated by industrial-era thinking. And yet most Americans are not aware that a particular form of the perennial philosophy, Freemasonry, has played an important role in the development of Western civilization and particularly the American democratic experiment. The philosophy that underlies Freemasonry has gone by many names since its origin in the Egyptian mystery religions. In the latter half of the 18th century, Freemasonry played a leading role in the emergence of democratic philosophies of government.

Freemasonry as it existed at that time was both esoteric and political (in contrast to contemporary Masonic lodges, which are much more in the nature of social organizations). The essential premise of Freemasonry was that there exist transcendental realms of reality, patterns, and forces. While these realms are inaccessible to the physical senses, they play important roles in shaping evolutionary and human events. These realms are capable of being explored by looking into the deep mind, and the knowledge gained thereby can be tested in much the same way knowledge acquired through the senses is tested—by comparing it with the observations of others, by seeing how it reconciles with one's coherent picture of "how things are," as derived from other experience (rational as well as intuitive and aesthetic), and by seeing whether what it implies about the future checks with further observations.

The Freemasonry network of the 18th century transcended national boundaries; there were members in Great Britain, France, and Poland, as well as America. Freemasonry was concerned with more than the development of individual awareness; most particularly, its concern focused upon the development of human knowledge and the arts and the reformation of governments toward a "philosophic commonwealth" and democratic forms.

Every American carries with him a symbolic reminder of Freemasonry's contribution to our own democracy, in the reproduction, on the back of the dollar bill, of the Great Seal of the United States. The design of the Great Seal was chosen in 1782, although there have been various minor modifications since then. (Considerable opposition was expressed to the decision in 1935 to place on the currency this "dull emblem of a Masonic fraternity," as Professor Charles Eliot Norton called it.) If one imagines that the founders of the United States were a motley citizenry of farmers, shopkeepers, and country gentlemen, the Great Seal symbols seem a puzzling choice, coming as they do from the ancient traditions of Freemasonry and tracing back thousands of years. But Benjamin Franklin and George Washington were both active and high-ranking Freemasons. Of the 56 signers of the Declaration of Independence, approximately 50 were Masons. All but five of the 55 members of the Constitutional Convention were Masons. Many Freemasons from other countries supported the American Revolution, including Lafayette, Kosciusko, Baron de Kalb, and Count Pulaski. Offshoots of the secret Masonic societies of Europe were transplanted to the New World 15 years before the American Revolution, at least in part with the express purpose of initiating a democratic experiment that had not found fertile soil in Europe.

The symbolism of the Great Seal portrays a particular vision of the future. This vision not only sustained and guided this nation during most of its 200-year history, but also for a time provided inspiration to the poor and downtrodden around the world. It no longer does either. America's vision of the future is neither clear to itself nor inspiring to

others. For that reason it is important to remind ourselves of what this vision once meant.

Bearing in mind that the essence of a powerful symbol is that it says many things to many levels of the mind (so that any explanation of its meaning is necessarily a dilution and a distortion), let us examine the symbolism of the Great Seal.

The most conspicuous Masonic symbol in the Great Seal is the unfinished pyramid capped by a radiant triangle enclosing the All-seeing Eye, which occupies the center of the reverse side of the seal. Whatever other meanings this ancient symbol may have (e.g., significance is attached to the numbers of levels and stones and to the resemblance to the great Pyramid of Gizeh, the shrine tomb of Hermes, personification of Universal Wisdom), it clearly proclaims that the works of men (either the individual's character or external works) are incomplete unless they incorporate divine insight. This symbol indicates that the nation will flourish only as its leaders are guided by supraconscious intuition.

The phrase *novus ordo seclorum* (from Vergil), meaning "A new order of the ages is born," declares that this event is not just the formation of another nation but of a new order for the world. The project is launched with confidence because *annuit coeptis*, "He [God] looks with favor upon our undertaking."

Dominating the obverse of the seal is the bird that is now an eagle, but in earlier versions was the Phoenix, the ancient symbol of human aspiration toward universal good, of being reborn through enlightenment and higher awareness. The olive branch and arrows in the bird's claws announce that the new order covets peace but intends to protect itself from those who would destroy it.

E pluribus unum, "unity from many," refers to the nation made up of states; probably also to the higher unity. The star-studded glory over the bird's head traditionally symbolizes the cosmic vision.

A Conflict in Premises

Modern Western man is suspicious of such a transcendental outlook as these symbols present—first, because it does not seem to be grounded in publicly verifiable perceptions as in science; second, because it is difficult to distinguish from superstitious nonsense; and third, because it seems to connote some sort of quietistic retreat from the problems of the world.

The first objection is gradually being countered by science itself, as it is becoming apparent that the divisions between subjective and objective, observer and observed, are nowhere near as clear-cut as had been assumed in the early naive period of science-versus-religion debates. Because the deep-rooted attitudes and repressions of the observer affect his observations, the same problem of discerning what knowledge is public, universal, and therefore "true" permeates all of science, though it is more obviously troublesome in some fields than in others.

The second ground for suspicion, the difficulty of communication, is fundamental. Because ordinary perception as experienced is a partial perception (from this broader outlook, at any rate), the language and metaphors built up from ordinary perception prove inadequate to describe the expanded view of reality. Hence such attempts sound paradoxical.

As to the third objection, to be sure, some versions of the perennial philosophy do sound like a quietistic retreat, at least in their Western interpretations. Part of society's negative reaction to monistic and Eastern kinds of beliefs, as these have appeared in the hippie counterculture and various contemporary cults, has been due to the fear that they would lead to dropping out, withdrawal, and passivity and therefore would undermine the social structure. From this standpoint, one of the most important characteristics of the Freemasonry interpretation is the central role it gives to creative work.

But if there are doubts about the suitability of the old guiding symbols, there are surely doubts about whether we are presently being guided by any compass at all. Ever-increasing material consumption and waste is not an adequate "central project." Some contemporary observers claim that signs of the decline of American democracy, indeed of Western civilization, have been clearly visible for at least 60 years, and present problems and crises manifest the acceleration of that decline. Others remain more sanguine that the old system can be patched up and made to run satisfactorily.

It is at least sobering, if not alarming, to note that (abetted by a deep-seated unemployment anxiety) we feel constrained to consume energy ever faster in a sort of drunken addiction; to make excessive demands on natural storehouses of minerals and fossil fuels, on the capacity of the physical environment to absorb the wastes of industrialized society, and on the resiliency of the planet's life-support systems to massive insults; to continue on a course of action which the majority of the world's population are increasingly viewing as exploitative of the earth's resources to satisfy the voracious appetites of the few. Lack of a sense of significant goals contributes to an inflation that threatens the stability of the economy.

The American symbols that once were the source of hope to oppressed peoples all over the world have become the symbols of the oppressor; the American dream has developed nightmarish overtones. Nor is it, of course, confined to this country. The whole industrialized world, intoxicated with the trappings of a materially extravagant society, is equally bereft of a sense of direction. *The fundamental dilemma is worldwide, but in this nation (because of the circumstances of its origin) it assumes a unique form—and presents a unique opportunity.*

The fundamental symbols and traditions of this nation point to a real, knowable, transcendent realm of experience leading toward individual commitments, cultural values, and national goals. This component of human experience was one of the foundations of American ideals and institutions. The concept of a transcendental, choosing, ultimately responsible self is central to the entire theory of democratic government. It underlies the assumption that the individual (despite his or her early conditioning) is finally responsible for a criminal act. It is basic to the assumption in the judicial process that the judge can make a meaningful judgment. It was assumed in Adam Smith's notion of the "invisible hand" that guides the capitalist system.

The specific symbols associated with the nation's birth have an additional significance. It is under these symbols, principles, and goals, properly understood, *and no others*, that the differing viewpoints within the nation can ultimately become reconciled. Only then can the nation once again become unified around a paramount "central project." The conservatives will insist that we retain and respect these national foundations. And radical youth will insist that we live up to them.

Instruments of Power by Thomas Hart Benton

CHAPTER EIGHT

THE TRANSINDUSTRIAL ERA

FOR SCORES OF YEARS the industrial-era paradigm led us to anticipate continued and inevitable material progress. America's view of the future was thoroughly positive. Conquer geographical and then interplanetary frontiers; pursue ever more wondrous technological achievements; spread prosperity and democracy around the world. The goals were clear and inspiring, and the motivation unflagging. It was inconceivable that the rest of the world might not want to follow in America's footsteps.

But this image of the future didn't survive the journey. As psychologist Kenneth Keniston notes in *The Uncommitted*, "Our visions of the future have shifted from images of hope to vistas of despair; Utopias have become warnings, not beacons. Huxley's *Brave New World*, Orwell's *1984* and *Animal Farm*, Young's *The Rise of the Meritocracy*, and ironically even Skinner's *Walden Two*—the vast majority of our serious visions of the future are negative visions, extensions of the most pernicious trends of the present." Material progress, the central goal of industrial society, has been transmuted into pollution, energy shortage, and problems of uncontrolled growth. Affluence and leisure have been gained, but with them have come persistent unemployment and worker discontent. The promise of technological miracles has come to look more like the problem of technology control. The rising standard of living somehow turned into the spectacle of the well-fed few and the starving many.

The chrome-and-plastic, jet-propelled image of future progress has run into difficulties. We currently live without the benefit of powerful positive myths, symbols, and images of the future. The industrial system has immense drive but is out of control; no clear and satisfactory guiding images and goals remain to give it direction. This lack of a beacon to steer toward could be fatal. As Dutch scholar Fred Polak says in *The Image of the Future*, "Any student of the rise and fall of cultures cannot fail to be impressed by the role played in this historical succession by the image of the future. The rise and fall of images precedes or accompanies the rise and fall of cultures. As long as a society's image is positive and flourishing, the flower of culture is in full bloom. Once the image begins to decay and lose its vitality, however, the culture does not long survive." Discovery of a suitable guiding image of the future is clearly our society's most crucial task.

A Brief Recapitulation

What are the dynamics by which one guiding image of the future replaces another? What are the social forces that could produce such a transformation, and to what extent are they controllable? Can we now discern the essential characteristics of the new social paradigm and the new image of the future? Before we turn our attention to these matters, it is helpful to bring together, in the form of two premises, what has been said thus far.

1. *An interrelating set of fundamental dilemmas of industrial society, growing steadily more pressing, seems to require for its ultimate resolution a drastically changed social paradigm.* We seem able to tolerate neither the ecological consequences of continued material growth nor the economic consequences of a sudden stoppage. We fear the implications of greatly increased control of technological development and application, yet sense that such control is imperative. We recognize the fatal instability of economic nationalism and a growing gap between rich and poor nations, yet seem completely unable to turn the trend around. We seem unable to resolve the discrepancy between man's apparent need for creative, meaningful work and the economic imperatives that cause much human labor to become superfluous or reduce it to make-work.

2. *There are increasingly evident signs of the emergence of a new image of man, transcendent, with potentialities limited only by his beliefs, at once an individual propelled to seek increasing awareness and yet, in the depths of his being, already one with the awareness he seeks.* It is a new image of man in the sense that it challenges both the

dominant scientific world view that has evolved over the past few centuries and also the image of materialistic economic man that became enshrined in the institutions and economic theories of the industrial era. Yet this image of man is not new, since traces of it can be found, going back for thousands of years, in the core experiences underlying the world's many religious doctrines, as reported through myths and symbols, holy writings, and esoteric teachings. The durability and power of the new image of man is suggested by the fact that it reactivates the cultural and religious myths and symbols whose meaning had become forgotten, and that it seems to be substantiated by the further advances of the science which earlier played a role in seemingly discrediting it.

A More Fundamental Anomaly

There is a still more fundamental anomaly underlying the four dilemmas of growth, work, control, and distribution. It is that those problems are so deeply rooted in the basic industrial-era paradigm, and so intertwined with one another, that they are probably not resolvable, individually or together, within that paradigm. Thus:

The basic paradigm that has dominated the industrial era (including emphasis on individualism, free enterprise, and material progress; with social responsibility primarily the concern of the government; and with few restraints on capital accumulation, etc.),

• and that involves striving toward such goals as efficiency, productivity, continued growth of production and consumption, continued growth of technological and manipulative power,

• has resulted in processes and states (e.g., extreme division of labor and specialization, cybernation, stimulated consumption, planned obsolescence and waste, exploitation of common resources, alienation of persons from community and nature, etc.),

• which end up counteracting human ends (e.g., enriching work roles, resource conservation, environmental enhancement, equitable sharing of the earth's resources).

The result is a cultural crisis of major proportions—*a growing and massive challenge to the legitimacy of the present industrial system.*

The Great Legitimacy Challenge

From the perspective of history, the mightiest force for social change is the unproclaimed power of the society's citizens to challenge and withdraw legitimacy from any or all of the society's institutions. Familiar examples in the brief history of the United States include the challenge to the legitimacy of monarchical government in the Declaration of Independence, the withdrawal of legitimacy from the institution of slavery, the labor unions' successful challenge to the legitimacy of business treating workers as its property and, perhaps most remarkable of all, the complete withdrawal of legitimacy from the institution of political colonialism since World War II. Over the past ten or 15 years we have witnessed a growing challenge to the legitimacy of the present social system of the industrialized world—particularly to its economic, political, technological, industrial, corporate, and scientific aspects. This challenge may mark one of the most important events in the history of human civilization. More than by any other thing, the future will be shaped by how that legitimacy challenge is resolved.

Although its nature is not even clear to many of those people participating in it, this legitimacy challenge is identifiable by a number of signs:

- Third World insistence on a new international economic order.
- Environmentalist, consumer, minority rights, women's liberation, and youth protest movements.
- Criticisms of industrial products, business practices, and manipulative advertising.
- Survey data showing values and attitudes that imply need for change in the old order.
- Growing sense that old answers no longer work.
- Indications of disenchantment with the assumption that all scientific and technological advance is unqualifiedly good.
- Decreased trust in institutions of business and government.
- New labor demands for meaningful work and participation in management decisions.
- Increasing signs of alienation from work and from the non-communities called cities and suburbs.
- Evidence of widespread search for transcendental meanings to provide a sense of "what is worth doing."

Each factor in its own way contributes to challenging the legitimacy of a system that increasingly falls short of achieving the humane goals it espouses.

The ultimate power of such a threat to withdraw legitimacy is largely unrecognized. Major historical transformations often seem to stem from values and beliefs changing at a different pace from, and getting out of step with, changes in the sociopolitical structure. A challenge to the legitimacy of dominant institutions may follow, culminating in major institutional changes in the society. In comparative studies of historical revolutionary social change (such as the fall of the Roman Empire; the Protestant Reformation; the Industrial Revolution; the Western political revolutions in England, America, and France; the communist revolution in Russia; etc.), it comes to light that there have rather consistently been certain advance indications that appeared one to three decades before the major change became apparent. These lead indicators include:

- Alienation, purposelessness, lowered sense of community.
- Increased rate of mental disorders, violent crime, social disruptions, use of police to control behavior.
- Increased public acceptance of hedonistic behavior (particularly sexual), of symbols of degradation, of lax public morality.
- Heightened interest in noninstitutionalized religious activities (e.g., cults, revivals, secret practices).
- Signs of anxiety about the future, economic inflation (in some cases).

The similarity to news stories of the past decade hardly needs pointing out.

Legitimacy of a social system and its power concentrations is fundamentally based on its (1) being duly constituted, (2) adherence to adequate guiding moral principles, and (3) effectiveness in achieving agreed-upon goals. The contemporary challenge to our social order involves all three bases.

The governments of the industrialized democracies are clearly duly constituted. However, there exist other concentrations of power that are not so constituted, the main example being the tremendous power inherent in the world network of multinational corporations and financial institutions. Because of their widespread influence, these gigantic organizations are quasi-public. As the largest corporations have grown to wield influences over human lives that are comparable to those of governments, similar demands are being made of them that have historically been made of governments—demands that they assume responsibility for the welfare of those over whom they wield power. Among those who feel themselves to be disfranchised by their lack of representation in institutions of power are members of nonindustrialized nations, minorities, consumers, youth, the elderly, and women. On a separate front, the intellectual power of the scientific-technological establishment is being contested. Science's position as the ultimate arbiter of truth is challenged on the grounds that it is guided and dominated by prediction-and-control values that serve industrialism rather than by humanistic goals that enhance man.

Secondly, the challenge is made that the industrial system is not guided by adequate moral principles, particularly in the matter of equitable distribution of the earth's resources. Especially with regard to food, energy, and economic resources, the poor continue to get poorer relative to the rich nations. The industrial system possesses no effective ethic or mechanism of redistribution; economic incentives predominate over all. The system provides no effective ecological ethic; consumers often feel manipulated and defrauded. The sense of pride in striving toward noble goals seems clearly to be dwindling; the system does not foster goals that enlist the deepest loyalties and commitments of citizens.

And, thirdly, the charge is made that the system is proving ineffective in achieving even its own declared goals. The successes of technology and industrialization themselves appear to be primary causes of contemporary problems. The labor of the poor and unskilled is rendered of little value, and there is a lack of sufficient satisfying work roles. The system does not foster preservation of the planet's habitability or enhancement of the environment's capacity to promote the total health of individuals. Incentive structures of the industrial system fail to insure that future generations will have fossil and mineral resources and clean air, land, and water.

The strength of this three-pronged challenge is difficult to assess. Conceivably the problems might be alleviated to the extent that the legitimacy challenge would weaken and disappear. But if the challenge continues to grow, several outcomes could occur. The challenge could become sufficiently alarming that a highly authoritarian regime would arise and put it down by strong governmental action. Or the challenge could become much stronger and result in a major whole-system transformation.

In the middle of the 18th century it would have seemed preposterous to suggest that monarchies, with their preponderant military and financial power, would bow to a form of government "deriving its just powers from the consent of the governed." Yet, the same forces that inexorably brought about the development of modern democratic governments and overthrew colonial rule may now be at work in modern economies. We are moving toward business "of the people, by the people, and for the people"—business "deriving its just powers" from the consent of all those whose lives are affected by it.

Similarly, the proposition put forth in the preceding chapter, that a profound and rapid change in the dominant image of man is taking place, may seem unlikely—as unlikely as the Christianization of Rome might have seemed in the Third century. But, it may also be as accurate.

If the occurrence of an impending transformation is problematic, it would seem that the form of the new transindustrial paradigm must be even more uncertain. Yet, we actually can postulate quite a bit about the new social paradigm from the requisite attributes that (1) it must make the four dilemmas of the industrial era seem more resolvable, and (2) it must be compatible with the emerging new image of man.

Thus, let us examine five aspects of the new social paradigm toward which these attributes point: (1) a new image of man, (2) a new knowledge paradigm, (3) a new "central project" for the society, (4) institutional changes, and (5) new system incentives.

A New Image of Man

That the transindustrial society will be characterized by a new image of man has been emphasized already. From the new image we derive two important *ethics* and a revolutionary concept of *choice*; each of these aspects calls for more detailed examination.

The ecological ethic. If man identifies with the whole of nature, if he perceives that he is one with the vast community represented by the planet and all its life forms and with the vast evolutionary processes in time, he is naturally drawn to an ecological ethic, which relates his own self-interest to that of fellow man and future generations and to all life on the planet. Such an ecological ethic recognizes limitations on available resources, including space, and realizes that man is an integral part of the natural world, inseparable from it and the laws which govern it. It calls for man to act in partnership with nature in protecting the complex life-support systems of the planet, in husbanding resources appropriately, in modifying ecological relationships wisely, in reestablishing satisfactory recycling mechanisms in harmony with natural ones, and in moving toward a new equilibrium economic-ecological system wherein the distinction is more clear which kinds of growth are wholesome and which are cancerous.

Society's commitment to an ecological ethic is essential if the earth is to remain habitable. Such an ethic has been advocated many times in the past by both ancient and modern philosophers, from Lao-Tse through St. Francis to Mahatma Gandhi. Its basic tenets correspond to the prescientific assumptions of many so-called primitive peoples.

It is an ethic that is supported not only by modern scientific understanding of the requirements for continued human life on earth, but also by most known cultural and religious systems.

The self-realization ethic. Just as the perennial philosophy implies an ecological ethic, it also entails an ethic of self-realization. This ethic affirms that the proper end of all individual experience is the further growth in individual awareness and the evolutionary development of the human species; hence, the appropriate function of social institutions is to create environments that will foster this development. As with the ecological ethic, this ethic too is supported by modern scientific understanding (specifically psychotherapy and the newly emerging humanistic psychology) and is found at the core of almost all the religious philosophies the world has known.

Self-realization provides the most satisfactory answer to the alienation and anomie that currently surface as rebellion against industrial and bureaucratic practices that diminish man, as anxiety that we have somehow lost control of human affairs, and in efforts to regain satisfaction from work. Self-realization will be a necessary theme in the restructuring of social institutions to satisfy individuals' fundamental desire for self-determination and their need for full and valued participation in society. It will call for less centralized social decision making than now occurs and fewer bureaucratic approaches to accomplish social tasks.

These two ethics, one emphasizing the total community of man in nature and the oneness of the human race, and the other placing the highest value on developing one's own self, are not conflicting but complementary—two sides of the same coin. Together they leave room for both cooperation and wholesome competition, for love of others and for one's own individuality. Each is a corrective against excesses or misapplications of the other.

To thus state the ethics derived from the new image of man is to risk underemphasizing that what is of import is the form and strength of the inner dynamic giving force to those ethics. The two ethics as abstract principles have been around for many centuries, but only for brief periods in relatively small societies have they ever been institutionalized as the dominant guiding principles. Even then, their force has probably been much more a matter of authoritarian persuasion than of independent verification through inner experience.

The point is important because, as we must emphasize, the perennial philosophy is *not* an intellectually held belief system. It is an identification with the center of highest consciousness discoverable in one's own inner experience and a dis-identification with all else that is not that center—*my* body, *my* thoughts, *my* feelings and emotions, *my* specific desires. From this point of view the fundamental flaw in modern industrial society is the extent to which it discourages this self-discovery and identification. Instead of promoting the discovery that in the deepest part of oneself one wants to live an ecological and self-realization ethic, it fosters denial of and alienation from that deeper self. This fundamental wrongheadedness generates both the materialism that underlies the consumption-and-waste ethic and the confusion about worthy social goals. It also produces a basic fear of loss of control—either by losing one's mind (manifested in industrial society's anxiety over ecstasy in any form: sexual, drug-induced, or mystical), or by losing one's existence (evident in a death phobia that shows up most clearly in awkward avoidance of the subject).

Supraconscious choice. The concept of an ethic is inseparable from the process by which the individual chooses what attitudes and behaviors to espouse. When we use the word *choice* we usually mean ordinary conscious choice—deliberately choosing to act in certain ways and not in other ways. But we also know, since Sigmund Freud, that we choose subconsciously as well. We avoid recognizing threatening information; we repress certain memories, and respond to situations in accordance with the dictates of an authoritarian inner voice (which Freudian psychologists call the *super-ego*, behavioralists call *conditioning*, and we commonly think of as *conscience*).

Recognition of the power of this subconscious choosing has influenced not only the practice of psychotherapy, but most aspects of society. Thus, court sentences for criminals and society's attempts to rehabilitate them are both influenced by the belief that criminality is mainly a consequence of subconscious choices made very early in life. Early educational theories and practices are based in part on the assumption that unfavorable early environments may render children handicapped by unfortunate subconscious choices. Welfare policy and social work practices are influenced by the theory that welfare recipients are not inherently lazy but are victims of bad subconscious choosing. To draw a parallel, if an image of man "making subconscious choices" has influenced society's institutions and policies, so likewise may the concept implicit in the new image of man, of persons "making supraconscious choices."

Everyone is familiar to some extent with experiences that might be said to involve supraconscious choice. We usually speak of them as intuition, hunches, creative imagination, aesthetic judgment, and so on. One senses a "higher self"—a part of the self somehow above the level of the ordinary ego-self—exerting behind-the-scenes guidance. There

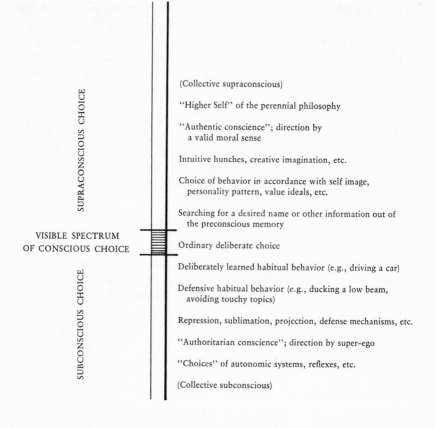

SUPRACONSCIOUS CHOICE

(Collective supraconscious)

"Higher Self" of the perennial philosophy

"Authentic conscience"; direction by
a valid moral sense

Intuitive hunches, creative imagination, etc.

Choice of behavior in accordance with self image,
personality pattern, value ideals, etc.

Searching for a desired name or other information out of
the preconscious memory

VISIBLE SPECTRUM
OF CONSCIOUS CHOICE

Ordinary deliberate choice

Deliberately learned habitual behavior (e.g., driving a car)

Defensive habitual behavior (e.g., ducking a low beam,
avoiding touchy topics)

Repression, sublimation, projection, defense mechanisms, etc.

"Authoritarian conscience"; direction by super–ego

"Choices" of autonomic systems, reflexes, etc.

SUBCONSCIOUS CHOICE

(Collective subconscious)

Figure 7. Spectrum of types of human choice.

are kinds of psychotherapy where the existence of some sort of higher self is assumed, as in Jungian analysis or psychosynthesis. The object of such therapy is, in effect, to align conscious choice with the highest discernible supraconscious choice, in which case the subconscious choices, too, will tend to follow.

The diagram of a "spectrum" of types of human choices (see *Figure* 7) illustrates the basic concept, suggesting how the narrow "visible spectrum" of conscious choice is bounded by vast ranges of subconscious and supraconscious choice.

Were the concept of supraconscious choice with all its implications to become as accepted a part of our social sciences and our culture as has the concept of subconscious processes, we might expect to see profound changes in our institutions and many of our public policies—just as we saw many changes when Freudian insights won high acceptance. The greatest impact would probably be in education. Training for socially useful employment would merge with education that builds self-awareness. Work, play, and learning would coalesce. The search for understanding that is science, the quest for wholeness that is psychotherapy, the reach for relationship that is religion, and the unfolding of potentialities that is education would be reunited, somewhat as they were in ancient Greece and in Europe during the Middle Ages. Ultimately national and world governments could come to depend upon supraconscious guidance, just as the founders of this nation so clearly believed their efforts were guided by a supraconscious force.

A New Knowledge Paradigm

A new image of man of course implies a new knowledge paradigm. That is to say, there would be drastic alterations in the nature of scientific inquiry, both in the subjects examined and the methods used. Many areas once considered strictly off limits for science would become not just *legitimate* fields for investigation, but *essential* fields of investigation. More importantly, the values implicit in the methodologies would be different.

It is not easy to appreciate what a profound change this would involve. Present-day science is primarily shaped by the industrial-era paradigm. Its aim is prediction and control, in both the physical and psychological realms of experience. The new science would aim toward vastly different goals, namely to guide individuals and society in their efforts to discover new realms of experience and potentiality and to foster actively the growth and evolution of society and individuals. The priorities, methods, and the overall cultural role of such a science would be very different from today's. Instead of being an eager servant of industry and the military, the new science would actively assist society in formulating new dominant goals for the whole culture.

By becoming broader in scope, the new science would reduce and perhaps even bridge the gap now separating what C.P. Snow calls the "two cultures"—science and technology at one extreme and the humanities and religion at the other. As discussed in the previous chapter, this new knowledge paradigm would encompass subjective as well as objective experience, entering domains previously the realm of religion, philosophy, literature, and the arts. It would not be reductionistic in its quest for "explanations," but would recognize, for instance, that a teleological cause may complement rather than contradict a mechanistic cause. Similarly, the new science would recognize various levels or realms of consciousness, acknowledging that concepts and metaphors appropriate to one mode or level (e.g., supraconscious) do not necessarily fit together at another level (e.g., conscious). It would accommodate the fact that men behave in some respects like conditioned automatons, but partake of the godlike as well.

The new science would also develop new methodologies. The controlled experiment would not be considered the only way to arrive at truth. The new science would foster open, participative inquiry; it would diminish the dichotomy between observer and observed, investigator and subject. Investigations of subjective experience would be based on collaborative trust and "exploring together," rather than on the sort of manipulative deception that has characterized much past research in the social sciences. And this new science would be fundamentally a *moral* rather than a *value-free* inquiry. It would investigate which values are wholesome for man (much in the sense that the science of nutrition attempts to determine which foods are wholesome for man). It would give highest priority to exploring those deepest experiences from which societies and individuals derive their most basic value commitments and from which the noblest visions of human civilization have sprung. (This would not be in a reductionist sense, "explaining" them in terms of childhood conditioning or sublimated appetites, but rather in the intuitive-aesthetic sense of coming to understand them better in their own terms.)

A New Central Project

Every society has some dominant theme, some set of objectives that the citizenry understands and supports and that gives purpose to their social participation—some "central project," to use Etzioni's term. The central project that dominated the industrial era was material progress, especially technological progress. It was accepted and was seldom even questioned until the 1960s. According to various estimates, technological change has been responsible for from 60 to 90 percent of economic growth. The direction of technological change depends in the short run largely on perceived opportunities for earning a profit; over the longer run it depends upon the state of scientific knowledge, which develops haphazardly with the accretion of many small bits of knowledge from many independent sources. Thus, all technological change has been essentially unplanned and unregulated. As mentioned earlier, a technological imperative has governed—any technology which *could be* developed and applied to making a profit *was* developed and applied. If problems came up afterward—well, the government could worry about that. It is no wonder that disenchantment with material progress as a guiding purpose has been increasingly visible in recent years.

A new social objective is suggested by the new image of man and the ecological and self-realization ethics. Perhaps a useful model is to be found in Robert Hutchins' *The Learning Society*, in which, as Hutchins describes, learning, fulfillment, and becoming human are the primary goals and "all its institutions [are] directed to this end. This is what the Athenians did. . . . They made their society one designed to bring all its members to the fullest development of their highest powers. . . . Education was not a segregated activity, conducted for certain hours, in certain places, at a certain time of life. It was the aim of the society. . . . The Athenian was educated by the culture, by Paidea." Paidea was the educating matrix of the society; its highest and central theme was the individual's "search for the Divine Center."

We do not live in the time of the ancient Greeks, and we will not simply repeat their pattern. The transindustrial society will have cybernetic machines instead of slaves, and it may very likely have a deliberate concern with shaping the future that would have been alien to the Greek culture. In the transindustrial society, helping to choose the future may be one of the more important roles played by the citizenry.

Thus, our particular version might be a "learning and planning society" whose central project would be (1) promoting individual growth in awareness, creativeness, adaptability, curiosity, wonder, and love; (2) evolving social institutions to more effectively foster such individual growth; and (3) participating as a partner with nature in the further evolution of the human species on earth.

Learning in the broadest sense—including education, research, exploration, and self-discovery—and planning—participating in the community of concerned citizens to make a better future—are two activities that contribute to human fulfillment and social betterment. They are humane, nonpolluting, and nonstultifying; they can absorb unlimited numbers of persons not required for other sorts of work. This last capability is clearly a prime consideration in light of the need for more creative occupations. A key concern for the future is what work people are to be involved in when only part of the population, and only a fraction of those individuals' time, will be necessary to produce all the goods and services that the planet can tolerate and society can use.

Implicit in the learning and planning society is the replacement of the Protestant compulsive work ethic with a creative work ethic—what we could call a work-play-learn ethic. In this connection it is important to note the central role given to creative work in the Freemasonry version of the perennial philosophy. As one of its chroniclers, Manly P.

Hall, describes this central theme, "Man is given by Nature a gift—the privilege of labor. Through labor he learns all things. [The true] Mason is a builder of the temple of character. He is the architect of a sublime mystery—the gleaming, glowing temple of his own soul. He best serves God when he joins with the Great Architect in building more noble structures in the universe below."

Institutional Changes

If the learning and planning society is to come into being, it will need new or at least greatly altered institutions to carry out its two basic functions. Fundamental changes will have to occur throughout, but particularly in large corporations and financial organizations in order to bring their operative goals into closer alignment with overall societal goals. Without such institutional changes individuals would typically find themselves under pressure to act contrary to their perceptions of what would be good for them and society.

A radically new kind of social responsibility in the private sector is the only alternative to continued expansion of the role of the public sector, and it may be the only alternative to a centrally planned economy. To say this is not to blame the corporations—there are no research findings showing that corporate managers and stockholders are more shortsighted or greedy or evil than the rest of humanity. Neither is it to imply that the corporations must do all the changing. *The whole system must change, and nothing less than that will meet the challenge of our time.* But the large corporations have a dominating influence in industrial society that makes them the crux of this transformation.

With considerable utility, we may think of society as having traditionally three main sectors—the private or business sector, the public or government sector, and the citizenry or voluntary sector. This simple model closely approximated reality prior to World War II. Social goals were set principally by the citizenry and secondarily by their elected representatives in government. The business sector responded to the marketplace with some regulation from government.

John Kenneth Galbraith, in *Economics and the Public Purpose*, described the profound change that occurred in the world economic system when the key components of the business sector, the large manufacturing and financial institutions, approached their present size (primarily in the period following World War II). According to Galbraith, the private sector divided into two parts that are quite different from one another. One part includes the 1,000 or so largest corporations, which Galbraith calls the "planning system," and the other is made up of the smaller corporations and businesses, which he calls the "market

Planning and Realization by Hans Erni

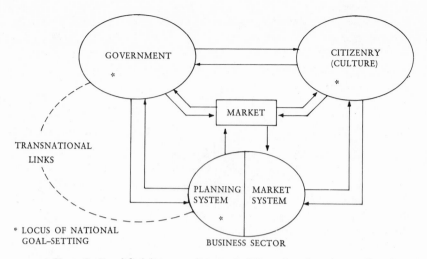

GOVERNMENT
*

CITIZENRY
(CULTURE)
*

MARKET

TRANSNATIONAL
LINKS

PLANNING
SYSTEM

MARKET
SYSTEM
*

* LOCUS OF NATIONAL
GOAL–SETTING

BUSINESS SECTOR

Figure 8. Simplified diagram of sectors in U.S. society (based on Galbraith).

system" (see *Figure 8*). The market system is still governed by economic forces of supply and demand (albeit with considerably more paperwork passing between the head office and Washington). But the corporate managements making up the planning system, together with the burgeoning bureaucracies in Washington to which they link ever more closely, are able to intervene in the market (and other areas as well) through the sheer power of the vast resources they command. Many of these corporations now control more wealth and have a higher annual production output than all but the few richest nations in the world. No longer are these mammoth multinational corporations simply subject to market forces; they exert control over the market through advertising, the products they make available, the materials they supply and consume, and so on. No longer are they simply subject to the controls imposed by national governments; in an important sense they exert control *over* national governments.

Thus, in our advanced industrial society, there is a new locus of goal-setting; goals are set not only by the citizenry and the government, but by corporate managers as well. These corporate managers are not elected by or representative of the people. Nor do they make decisions according to the same principles that guide the setting of national goals in government. The nation becomes, in a sense, a three-headed monster with diverse goals being pursued by each. Because of this situation, a demand has arisen that if the corporate structure is to be considered *legitimate* in playing a major role in determining national goals, it must somehow be responsible to all those affected by its actions.

There are several ways the situation might resolve itself. The government might assume the dominant role and bring the planning system decision making into line with the decisions of representative government in a sort of state capitalism. Or the government might reduce the power of the planning system in what some people call a "new socialism," which would involve greatly expanded government ownership and operation. A third possibility is that the planning system might become dominant. In this case the citizenry might accept the goals of corporations as those of the country—an exaggerated case of "what's good for business is good for the nation." Still another alternative, the one most in keeping with the ideals of representative democracy, would involve acceptance by corporate management of the claims of various publics to have the corporations responsible to them but would not involve government domination.

This last alternative is not as utopian or improbable as it may seem at first glance. To begin with, it is supported by logic. Stockholders, after all, represent only one group that has a major investment in the corporations. The employees invest a portion of their lives there, and the society invests in the corporations some measure of influence over its future. Furthermore, the vast majority of the population is in some ownership position (indirectly, in most cases, through pension plans, mutual funds, life insurance, etc.) and thus share in the investment. Expanded ownership plans making it easy for employees to acquire stock are being adopted by a number of corporations. Thus, large private corporations are becoming quasi-public. They are owned by the public, serve the public, and expose the public to the consequences of bad corporate behavior.

Already the courts are moving toward relaxation of corporations' responsibility to stockholders and extension of their fiduciary responsibility to the general public. Such legal rulings are a continuation of the trend in which fiduciary obligation has gradually broadened from primary responsibility to stockholders to those who work for the corporation, to those who buy from it, to those who supply it, and to those who lend to it. Courts have already held that human, scientific, capital, and natural resources are all imbued with a public interest, and that private property cannot be used for purposes that will destroy its utility for a higher use. This sort of ruling is another illustration of the fact that the ultimate power to grant or withdraw legitimacy rests with the people and that there are ways other than elected representation to insure the accountability of an institution to its ultimate constituency.

Thus, it may not be utopian but rather realistically practical, as further cultural changes take place, for the legitimate priority of corporate goals to become:

1. To provide satisfying and growth-fostering work for employees.
2. To contribute to the overall social welfare.
3. To engage successfully in economically profitable activities.

Those who participate in the corporation, as owners, employees, or customers, will do so through a wish to see these goals achieved. Profit, return on investment, and capital growth will remain important but they will not be exclusive goals; rather, they will serve as indicators of how effectively all the goals are being realized.

If the free-enterprise, democratic system, with all its very real advantages, is to avoid coming under oppressive government control, it will do so because the powerful business and labor organizations bring their goals into alignment with humane and farsighted societal goals. Particularly with regard to the redistributional problem of the rich and poor nations, new forms of world corporations, truly multinational in ownership and management, have a key role to play. Much will depend upon whether these large corporations assume an active responsibility for creating a healthy world society and a habitable planet, not as a gesture to improve corporate image or as a moralistically undertaken responsibility, but *because it is the only reasonable long-run interpretation of good business practice.* A new social contract is being written between large corporations and society. In the end, good business policy must become one with good social policy.

Still other institutional changes in the transformation to a learning and planning society include new opportunities for full citizen participation in the society and for lifelong learning, together with a general restructuring of all organizations to enhance rather than diminish man.

Full and valued participation in the society, available to each citizen, is becoming recognized as a fundamental political right. Every member of the society needs to know that he can, by his own efforts, have his economic needs met and make a contribution that will be judged to be worthwhile by society. For the majority this means structured jobs, which also implies that the government is the employer of last resort. But a growing fraction of the population will be capable of structuring its own activities. It will be to society's advantage to let these individuals function independently, thus opening up structured jobs for those with less imagination and self-reliance.

Full participation also means that every citizen must be able to contribute to decisions regarding social goals. Citizen participation in decision making is one of the most effective ways of stimulating socially responsible behavior—far more so than imposing restraints by means of governmental regulations. When given such responsibility, even quite ordinary individuals may be moved to broaden their horizons—to weigh seriously global as well as local concerns, future as well as present consequences. Such developments would be valued additions to trans-industrial society.

And of course citizens cannot develop or participate fully in a society unless they have opportunities to grow intellectually and emotionally. Lifelong learning must be fostered by all institutions—by the home and place of employment as well as by schools and the government. But education will probably become more individual than it is now, with students allowed more freedom to select their own subject areas and to proceed at their own speed and by their own means.

Many institutions today demand rigid economic efficiency or bureaucratic conformity from their employees—they are "factories" in the worst sense of the word. They would contribute more to human satisfaction if they functioned more like healthy families, accepting the need to be a nurturing community whose principal goal is to enhance the lives of its members. Such organizations would foster individual autonomy at the same time that they developed in each individual the sense of being an integral part of the whole.

Organizations such as this will still need hierarchies of responsibility, but leadership and responsibility may change with each new mission, and there should always be widespread participation in setting organizational goals. Decisions should be made at the lowest practicable level. The workplace would thus become a setting for satisfying and self-actualizing activity. Jobs would be shaped to the human needs of those who perform them, rather than people shaped to jobs whose form is dictated solely by considerations of economic efficiency. There would be economic incentives of course, but much more attention would be paid to other incentives which typically induce persons to contribute their best efforts—loyalty, a sense of responsibility, aesthetic gratification, the search for truth, and identification with common goals and the general welfare.

Truly enhancing institutions would have widespread effects. The present institutionalization of welfare—of social, medical, and educational services—yields seriously destructive by-products. We have yet to learn that better health is not more doctors, better education is not more teachers, and greater welfare is not more social workers. In the emerging social paradigm, organizations devoted to fostering health, education, and welfare would be restructured to enhance those they serve and to liberate people from dependence on such institutions.

New System Incentives

One of the most effective ways to bring about change in individual and organizational behavior without infringing on personal liberties is to provide economic incentives for desired behavior. Much of our present predicament can be traced to the fact that basic economic incentives run counter to socially desirable objectives. For instance, many methods of increasing corporate profits have undesirable ecological or social consequences, and short-term economic considerations often penalize future generations. But incentives can be established that help bring the actions of persons and corporations into line with society's needs.

The tax structure offers an obvious potential mechanism for applying such incentives. For example, a worldwide energy tax might be instituted, coupled with a redistribution mechanism to avoid penalizing the poorer countries, in order to conserve energy reserves for future generations. There would be numerous practical difficulties in reaching agreement on such a tax, but, if instituted, it would alter millions of people's perception of energy. Conservation would then offer clear-cut benefits. Such a tax would make it possible for individuals and institutions to afford to cut back their energy use. Previously they might have been convinced of the *desirability* of reducing their energy demands, but would not have made the effort without the incentive provided by the tax.

One can visualize changes in taxes and salary arrangements that would encourage frequent sabbatical leaves for those in the work force, and these leaves would in turn make jobs available for additional workers. A promising approach calls for certain taxes to be forgiven in order to stimulate the participation of private enterprise in fostering such sabbaticals while minimizing the amount of government direction. (One version has been used in France, to foster continuing education among employees.) This tax is levied on some appropriate measure of corporate activity, such as total payroll or gross income, but is subsequently "forgiven" provided that the money is used by the corporation for certain specified purposes, such as:

- Providing on-the-job education.
- Granting sabbatical or social-service leaves.
- Creating socially beneficial jobs (apprenticeships, youth employment, or post-retirement social service).
- Restructuring work to increase job satisfaction.

- Loaning managers to community services, or otherwise contributing to the solution of social problems.

New institutional forms may be required. One example might be the establishment of a proposed general-benefit or limited-profit corporation that would incorporate the vitality-promoting competitiveness of a profit-making corporation, the social purpose of a nonprofit corporation, and the personal-growth aims of a university. Another example might be an expanded-ownership corporation combining the goals and incentives of business and labor. Legislation revising antitrust and corporation laws and policy changes altering credit regulations could be used to encourage diverse kinds of organizational experiments and make them more economically attractive.

The possibilities for creative innovation are myriad. The guiding principle should be the one first noted by anthropologist Ruth Benedict. She observed that societies differ in a quality she called *synergism*. In a low-synergism society what the individual is naturally inclined to do tends to be at odds with what the society would have him do. In a highly synergistic culture, on the other hand, what the individual naturally wants to do tends to align with society's goals, and little coercion is required to bring about coordinated efforts. What we have been saying about incentives can be put in these terms. If the society is to become synergistic, incentives affecting individuals and institutions must be revised so that behavior consistent with ecological and self-realization ethics, which will presumably benefit society in the long run, is fostered instead of frustrated.

Metamorphosis of Narcissus by Salvador Dali

CHAPTER NINE

STRATEGIES FOR A VIABLE FUTURE

THE PRACTICAL MAN ASKS, "What can we do?" In partial response, we have proposed a guiding image of a transindustrial society. How do we know it will work? Before we discuss what kinds of strategies make sense, let us recapitulate briefly. In earlier chapters we have described four basic dilemmas of industrial society (involving growth, work roles, distribution, and technological control). It is clear that these dilemmas are so deeply intertwined that the resolution of any one depends upon the successful resolution of one or more of the others. Thus, when these problem areas are treated together, there appears to be a solution that otherwise is not possible.

The key to resolving the growth, work, distribution, and control dilemmas lies in the transformation to what we have called a transindustrial society. The transindustrial society would not automatically cure all our ills. Nor would it automatically overcome the widespread negative images of the future and the cultural crisis represented by the widespread alienation from and mistrust of the institutions of industrial society. (This cultural crisis, as described in Chapter Eight, manifests itself as a challenge to the legitimacy of the industrial-era paradigm.) It would be enough if the new paradigm made the whole collection of dilemmas and crises more solvable. This it appears to do. Thus, if we are correct in our prognosis, our questions become: How could this transindustrial society be brought into existence, and what strategies would ease the transition from our present industrial-era paradigm to the transindustrial paradigm?

Toward Resolution of the Basic Dilemmas

To emphasize the whole-system character of the resolution of these problem areas, we will key the discussion that follows to the matrix of *Figure 9*. This matrix illustrates the concept that a social system changes as an integrated organism. (The four dilemmas and the related cultural crisis are listed in the column at the left. The next column contains a brief statement indicating the nature of resolution for each problem area. The third column indicates how resolution of any one of the dilemmas depends at least indirectly on satisfactory progress toward resolution of one or more of the others. In turn, as shown in the final column, progress toward the satisfactory handling of any one of the problem areas contributes to the likelihood of resolving the others.)

One: The growth dilemma. The growth dilemma, for example, is ultimately resolved by movement toward a frugal society. Motivation for a frugal society involves commitment to an ecological ethic, which is an element of the new image of man described in Chapter Seven. The society, however, would not feel it could afford reduced material growth rates unless the work-roles dilemma were resolved. In addition to making the growth dilemma resolvable, the establishment of a frugal society would aid in solving the distribution dilemma (as indicated in Chapter Five). Furthermore, frugality with regard to resources would ease environmental impact problems and render the problem of technology control more manageable.

Proposals to "limit growth" and "reduce productivity" evoke a disapproving emotional response because the very phrases connote negativism if not defeat. But it is important that we realize that society need never limit productiveness and growth in human terms. Accordingly, as expressed earlier, the resolution of the growth dilemma lies in the movement toward a society that is highly productive in human terms and highly fostering of individual growth and development but frugal in its use of material resources.

Two: The work-roles dilemma. The work-roles dilemma is ultimately resolvable only through commitment to the basic political right of each citizen to opportunities for full and valued participation in the society as well as movement toward a learning and planning society. The problem of underemployment can be eradicated only through the existence of a meaningful "central project" to give purpose to relatively routine work.

Figure 9. A matrix showing the interrelating nature of society's fundamental dilemmas, and the requirement of whole-system change for eventual resolution.

Fundamental Dilemma	Nature of Resolution	Requires for Resolution	Resolution Would Contribute to
Growth	Movement toward a frugal society	Ecological ethic Resolution of the work dilemma	Resolution of distribution dilemma Easing of resource and environmental problems, hence of problems of technology management
Work roles	Commitment to full and valued participation as a fundamental political right Institutionalization of a learning and planning society	Self-realization ethic Meaningful "central project"	Resolution of growth dilemma Resolution of distribution dilemma
Distribution	More equitable distribution of the earth's resources Overlapping supranational institutions forming a planetary regulatory system (with important roles being played by the private and voluntary sectors)	Ecological ethic Movement toward a frugal society in the rich nations Resolution of the work dilemma	Reduction of world tensions and nuclear threat World stability Ability to deal more rationally with the growth dilemma
Control	Multi-level citizen participation network for technology assessment and management	Ecological ethic (to reduce tendency to approach problems in adversary mode)	Resolution of growth dilemma Resolution of the work dilemma
Cultural crisis (alienation, lack of agreed-upon goals, low trust in institutions)	Restructured society around a new image of man	Commitment to a new "central project"	Resolution of all four dilemmas

The economic function (income distribution) and the social function (self-development) of work need to be considered separately. A decreasing fraction of the work roles needed for either function arises naturally in the private sector operating in its normal profit-making mode, supplying needed goods and services. New ways of structuring socially desirable and individually self-fulfilling tasks are required—at least some in the nonprofit and voluntary sectors. And new mechanisms for income distribution need to be found.

Unless the main burden of providing these work roles is carried by the private and voluntary sectors, growth of a massive public service employment bureaucracy seems inevitable. We have earlier touched on cultural and incentive-system changes making it plausible that the workplace would come to be regarded as one of the main places where humans find their self-fulfillment. Efficiency in a narrow economic sense would become less of a dominating value, while such values as actualizing human potential, achieving community, and being socially responsible would assume greater importance. With these attitude changes there would be a redesigning of technology and the workplace to invest work with more meaning. Moreover, there would be job enrichment and reorganization of the work by the workers themselves to improve efficiency in a broad human sense—efficiency in developing and using human potential. Appropriate opportunities to participate and the therapeutic benefits of work would be provided to those whose capacity to contribute is low—the mentally and physically handicapped, those with a "failure" self-image, the elderly, and inexperienced youth. In somewhat the same way that the extended family used to take care of its own, the subunits of corporations would take on these sorts of broad community responsibilities.

To make this kind of behavior plausible within the corporation, we have to postulate both a significant cultural change (involving a strong espousal of the self-realization ethic) and supporting changes in incentive systems throughout the economy. The latter is necessary so that the corporation would not suffer economic disadvantage from accepting broad responsibility to provide "full humane employment." The "forgiven tax" mentioned in Chapter Eight is one such device; a graduated wage subsidy is another. (The wage subsidy is a way of raising to subsistence level wages for activities that are socially desirable but are not economically justified if the corporation has to pay the complete cost.) New types of corporations combining features of business, nonprofit organizations, and universities (e.g., a limited-profit corporation) offer other possibilities. The combination of cultural validation and incentive fostering would enable businesses to structure work to increase worker satisfaction, to provide broadly beneficial educational opportunities on and off the job, to provide apprenticeships and other youth employment opportunities, to design graduated entry pathways and special career paths for the unskilled and unmotivated, to release employees for sabbatical periods or social-service activities, to assist in mid-career changes of vocation, and to assist entrepreneurs in starting socially desirable new ventures.

If the work-roles dilemma could be satisfactorily resolved along these lines, this would remove much of the present paralysis with regard to the growth and distribution dilemmas; at present all sorts of otherwise constructive actions are precluded because of their impact on unemployment.

Three: The distribution dilemma. Redistribution among nations is another matter. Here there is no legitimated world government that could bring about such redistribution. The poor countries are plagued by monumental problems of unemployment and underemployment, brought about by labor-replacing technology and high population growth plus massive rural-urban migrations. More assistance from the rich countries, in amounts up to many tens of billions of dollars annually at least (still a small percentage of the gross product) will undoubtedly be necessary for survival of a world economic system and, indeed, of a world civilization.

New forms of world corporations, truly multinational in ownership and management, will probably play important roles here—at least as important as national governments and international agencies. They will be the key actors in the resolution of such fateful issues as the real opportunities for advancement available to underdeveloped nations, the distribution of resources among nations (e.g., whether pressures are placed on less-developed nations to sell their natural resources reserves preferentially, or unduly hastily), and the resistance of less-developed countries to environmental and materials-conserving policies that might slow down their rates of economic growth.

For the distribution dilemma to approach resolution, it would be necessary for world society to have developed a commitment to an ecological ethic, for the developed world to be moving in the direction of a frugal society, and for the work dilemma to be approaching resolution (otherwise helping to modernize the poorer nations would be too threatening to jobs in the wealthier countries).

Even so, we are talking about the distribution problems being resolvable, not resolved. It will take generations in some parts of the world before conditions of abject poverty can be altered satisfactorily. There can be no realistic hope of world stability until there is hope for the world's poor. Paradoxically, because part of the problem lies with the internal institutions of the poor countries, the route to global stability is likely to involve a fair amount of local political instability—but then, in view of our origins, Americans should understand that.

Four: The control dilemma. Satisfactory resolution of the dilemma of technology control requires a strong ecological ethic and agreement on the bases for making difficult trade-off decisions, substituting for the adversary mode of dealing with problems an attitude of "exploring together" for mutually satisfactory solutions. The long-term goals of the society need to be chosen in the political process, with effective citizen involvement and in the presence of as clear a knowledge as possible of the ways in which individual and corporate microdecisions combine to actualize or to thwart these goals. Cultural and institutional change will be involved in alignment of system incentives for the accomplishment of these goals.

There is thus at least some hope that man can learn to control his new Faustian powers over his physical and social environment. If the control dilemma were satisfactorily resolved, it would contribute directly to handling both the growth dilemma and the work-roles dilemma, and would reduce many of the instigating factors of our cultural crisis.

Five: The cultural crisis. The cultural crisis will not diminish until progress is evident with regard to the four basic dilemmas facing our society. Abatement of the cultural crisis depends upon the citizens joining together in a new meaningful central project. The existence of meaningful central goals would, in turn, go far toward lubricating the social machinery for dealing with the four dilemmas.

We have no way of anticipating the extent to which some of these changes might result in a powerful unleashing of motivation and dedicated energy. It is increasingly clear that human behavior, even in strictly economic institutions, is not governed by economic motivations to anywhere near the extent that used to be presumed in economic theory. We do not know how much more effectively business organizations might function if they were to restructure their operations and recast their themes to evoke that kind of identification with an enterprise, concern for its outcome, and sense of significant membership that have elicited, in other institutions such as the family and some voluntary associations, extraordinary amounts of conscientious giving of one's best, without thought or concern for differentiated rewards, economic or otherwise.

The image of a viable future is essential for successful passage through the years ahead. This image will have to embody an understanding of the interconnected nature of societal problems (as suggested in the matrix of *Figure 9*).

Strategies for a Nondisruptive Transition

To go further we will have to assume that the arguments up to now make sense, on the whole. That is, we need to postulate that the kind of transformation we have been describing, to a transindustrial society, seems both to be underway and to be desirable. We may envision the society as a great organism, which has come to a crisis period and is in process of healing itself, of making a transition into a new stage of life. At issue is how disruptive that transition is going to be. We now want to explore the kinds of strategies that seem appropriate *if* this transformational view is taken seriously.

We will concentrate on strategies for the United States. They would be similar for other parts of the industrialized world but with important differences, especially for the nations with planned economies. Significantly different strategies would be appropriate for those Third World nations with resources valued by the industrialized world; and they would be still more different for the remaining "Fourth World" nations with no resources other than poor land and poor people.

We assume, then, that the case for the dynamics of transformation being already present is plausible, and we address the question of *how to manage a nondisruptive transition*. Six elements of an overall strategy suggest themselves:

One: Promote awareness of the unavoidability of the transformation, as a first essential element of the strategy. Pulled by emergence of a new transcendentalism and pushed by the demonstrated inability of the industrial-era paradigm to resolve the dilemmas its successes have engendered, the fact and the shape of the necessary transformation are set in place. Growing signs of economic and political instability indicate that the time is at hand. No more than the pregnant woman approaching the time of her delivery can we stop and reconsider whether we really want to go through with it. But the extent of the transition's disruptiveness can still be affected by our degree of understanding. The time is ripe for a great dialogue in the national and world arena as to how we shall pass through the transformation, and toward what ends.

Two: Construct a guiding vision of a workable future society, built around the new image of man and the new social paradigm. As the old order shows increasing signs of breaking apart, some adequate vision of what may be simultaneously building is urgently needed to mobilize constructive effort that would facilitate an orderly transition to a new social order. It is self-evident that an effective image of a humane high-technology society, congenial to the new image of man, will have to be constructed. This new image of society needs to *evolve with full citizen participation*, not be designed by a technocratic elite or revealed by a charismatic leader. In attempting to describe some of the characteristics of the emerging society in the preceding pages, there should have been no illusion that we were preparing a blueprint. The new social paradigm, and the form of the transindustrial society, will emerge out of the creative process of many minds in interaction. Even now, though we can only dimly see the transindustrial paradigm taking form, we can already begin to identify some of the attributes a workable future society will have to embody.

Three: Foster a period of experimentation and tolerance for diverse alternatives, both in life-styles and social institutions. Experimentation is needed to find out what works, but there is a more important reason for trying to maintain an experimental climate—namely, to reduce hostile tensions between individuals who are actively promoting the new and those who are desperately attempting to hold on to the old. In public education, for instance, it is equally important that new experimental curricula be tried *and* that traditional subjects and methods of instruction continue to be available. Experimental communities are extremely important laboratories of the future, yet they should not encroach forcefully on the life-styles of the less venturesome.

Four: Encourage a politics of uprightness and morality in government and a heightened sense of public responsibility in the private sector. Surveys and polls display drastically lowered faith among the American people in both government and business. An atmosphere of trust is essential for the tasks ahead, however. Political leaders will need more than ever to demonstrate honesty and strength of purpose. (Such traits would be laudable in any generation, but they may be indispensable for safe passage through the times just ahead.) Moreover, the powerful private institutions must develop a greatly heightened sense of stewardship and public responsibility, if they expect to survive rising challenges to the legitimacy of large profit-seeking industrial corporations and financial institutions. If these are to be more than merely pious statements, changes in institutional arrangements and socioeconomic incentives will need to be instituted so that individuals can *afford* to behave in ways that further society's best interests.

Five: Promote systematic exploration of, and foster education regarding, man's inner life. Chapter Eight described an emerging scientific paradigm that places far more emphasis than in the past on exploring man's inner experiences. At present far too much societally important exploration into these areas must be conducted informally or illicitly. Interested persons of all ages resort to cultish associations, bizarre experimentation, or illegal drug use because they find legitimated opportunities for guided inner exploration to be inadequate, inappropriate, or inaccessible in society's religious, educational, scientific, and psychotherapeutic institutions. America's guarantee of religious freedom has been curiously subverted by the powerful orthodoxy of a materialistic scientific paradigm.

Six: Accept the necessity of social controls for the transition period while safeguarding against longer-term losses of freedom. The coming transformation has a paradoxical aspect. In considerable measure the emerging transformation has been brought about by the success of material progress (through better nutrition, a higher standard of living, more education, and mass communication) in raising a large proportion of the population above excessive concern with subsistence needs. However, economic decline and social disruptions that are very likely to occur during the transition period will tend to accentuate material "security" needs. Political tensions will rise and disunity will characterize social affairs. (Yes, far more than we have experienced to date.) Some regulation and restraint of behavior will be necessary in order to hold the society together while it goes around a difficult corner, somewhat as temporary restriction of freedoms had to be imposed during World War II. The greater the public understanding of the transitory but inescapable nature of this need, the greater the likelihood that a more permanent authoritarian regime can be avoided.

We can present no strategy of deliberate planning for a well-ordered transition. If the foregoing six strategic steps are taken seriously they represent a profound shift from present policies. If they offer something less than a grand design for the future society, perhaps they can contribute to a more orderly transformation and will leave fewer social wounds to be healed than would otherwise be the case.

Postlude

This discussion would not be complete without considering reasons why the transformation that has been postulated might *not* take place. Basically there are two possibilities. One is that the two forces we have identified—the pressure of unresolvable dilemmas and the emergence of a new image of man—may prove to be much weaker than we have assumed. In that case, the momentum of the long-term trend toward utilitarian, rational, industrial society would continue bringing us a future that would be a continuation of the past, but plagued with increasingly vexing social and environmental problems.

The second possibility is that the two forces for transformation are indeed present in strength but that the resistance to change proves to be too strong—in which case industrial society could enter a period of decline from which it would fail to recover.

The sources of such resistance are several. Most deeply rooted is individual and cultural resistance to change in our fundamental perceptions and premises. If indeed there exists a basic wrongheadedness with regard to institutions (in that those suitable for building up a vast technological-industrial apparatus are inadequate to the humane use of these new powers) and a basic wrongheadedness with regard to the dominant image of man (in that he is persuaded that he is less than he could discover himself to be), then experience suggests that disclosure of this error will be resisted mightily. As noted earlier, there is good reason to believe that society may resist the very knowledge it most needs to solve its problem, much as a patient in psychotherapy often avoids or resists the knowledge that could help him most.

Institutions have rigidity and inertia as well and tend to perpetuate the values and premises that have been built into them. For example, businesses long accustomed to exploiting the environment for economic gain through the production of goods and services would naturally tend to resist reorientation toward new outputs that would enhance the environment and create meaningful social roles. Moreover, there is realistic justification for such resistance. Because the whole society does behave more or less as an integrated organism, any single institution that attempts to move more rapidly than the rest of the system could accept would find itself in deep trouble.

Anxiety over change produces irrational and unconsciously motivated behavior opposing that change. If we lack sufficient understanding of the necessity for change and lack the vision of a positive future that is both desirable and attainable, we may respond inadequately—and quite incorrectly—to the challenges we face.

In the end, education is our only salvation—education of ourselves toward a fuller understanding of both the evolutionary leap mankind struggles to effect and the requirements for a successful transformation to the transindustrial society. All we have learned of psychotherapy suggests that it is at the precise time when the individual most feels as though his whole life is crashing down around him that he is most likely to achieve an inner reorganization constituting a quantum leap in his growth toward human maturity. Our hope, our belief, is that it is precisely when society's future seems so beleaguered—when its problems seem almost staggering in complexity, when so many individuals seem alienated, and so many values seem to have deteriorated—that it is most likely to achieve a metamorphosis in society's growth toward maturity, toward more truly enhancing and fulfilling the human spirit than ever before. Thus we envision the possibility of an evolutionary leap to a transindustrial society that not only has know-how, but also has a deep inner knowledge of what is worth doing.

Courtesy Hans Erni, Lucerne

Primitive Community by Hans Erni

READER'S GUIDE

At the end of this brief argument we attempt to suggest some further readings that may amplify or complement the discussion. In one sense the most pertinent supplementary reading is not yet written or published, because the events it deals with have not yet occurred. That is to say, the attempt here has been to identify a pattern for interpreting future events. The pattern fits the past reasonably well (although not uniquely); its usefulness depends on how well it helps anticipate and make sense of future developments. Having said that, I would like to single out a few writings that I have found useful, illuminating, or inspiring. The list is both selective and subjective.

In Chapter One several examples of future forecasts were mentioned. Among those predicting a future defined by projection of past trends are:

- Kahn, Herman and B. Bruce-Briggs. *Things to Come: Thinking About the '70s and '80s.* New York: Macmillan, 1972.
- Brzezinski, Zbigniew. *Between Two Ages: America's Role in the Technetronic Era.* New York: Viking Press, 1970.
- Bell, Daniel. *The Coming of Post-Industrial Society: A Venture in Social Forecasting.* New York: Basic Books, 1973.

On the other hand, the following see a humanistic transformation:

- Reich, Charles A. *The Greening of America: How the Youth Revolution is Trying to Make America Livable.* New York: Random House, 1970.
- Leonard, George B. *The Transformation: A Guide to the Inevitable Changes in Humankind.* New York: Delacorte, 1972.

Two authors in particular have discussed the evolutionary significance of the coming transformation:

- Platt, John R. *The Step to Man.* New York: Wiley, 1966.
- Boulding, Kenneth E. *The Meaning of the Twentieth Century.* New York: Harper, Colophon Books, 1964.

A more pessimistic view, seeing the necessity for a transformation in the future but doubting that world society can respond in time, is found in:

- Heilbroner, Robert. *An Inquiry into the Human Prospect.* New York: W.W. Norton, 1974.

For numerous articles about future problems and possibilities consult your library's files of *The Futurist* (Washington, D.C.: World Future Society).

Further elaboration of the transformation theme is found in Chapter Two. Drucker writes of the "discontinuities" of our time, Mumford compares the present with historical transformations, and Kuhn introduces the concept of dominant paradigm:

- Drucker, Peter. *The Age of Discontinuity*. New York: Harper and Row, 1968.
- Mumford, Lewis. *The Transformations of Man*. New York: Harper and Brothers, 1956.
- Kuhn, Thomas. *The Structure of Scientific Revolutions* (second edition). Chicago: University of Chicago Press, 1970.

Yankelovich presents evidence of value change in the society and Revel interprets the cultural revolution:

- Yankelovich, Daniel. *The Changing Values on Campus*. New York: Washington Square Press, 1972. Also *The New Morality: Profile of American Youth in the '70s*. New York: McGraw Hill, 1974.
- Revel, Jean-François. *Without Marx or Jesus*, trans. Bernard. New York: Doubleday, 1971.

Chapter Three discusses the growth dilemma. One of the first authors to point out in detail the difficulties to which technological growth ultimately leads was:

- Brown, Harrison. *The Challenge of Man's Future*. New York: Viking Press, 1954.

The nature of the dilemma is forcefully described in:

- Commoner, Barry. *The Closing Circle*. New York: Knopf, 1971.

Daly discusses the leveling off of economic growth and, in what bids fair to become the bible of the ecology movement, Schumacher describes the blessings of a society that has put economic growth in its place:

- Daly, H., ed. *Toward a Steady-State Economy*. San Francisco: W.H. Freeman, 1973.
- Schumacher, E.F. *Small is Beautiful: Economics as if People Mattered*. New York: Harper and Row, 1973.

On work, the subject of Chapter Four, the following are helpful supplements:

- Kelso, L.O. and Mortimer Adler. *The Capitalist Manifesto*. New York: Random House, 1958.
- Michael, Donald. *Cybernation: The Silent Conquest*. Santa Barbara: Center for the Study of Democratic Institutions, 1962.
- O'Toole, James, ed. *Work in America*. Cambridge: M.I.T. Press, 1973.
- Sheppard, Harold L. and R. Herrick. *Where Have All the Robots Gone?* New York: Free Press, 1972.

The problem of rich vs. poor nations as discussed in Chapter Five is treated in:

- Brown, Lester. *World Without Borders*. New York: Random House, 1972.
- Heilbroner, Robert. *The Great Ascent: The Struggle for Economic Development in Our Time*. New York: Harper and Row, 1963.
- Myrdal, Gunnar. *The Challenge of World Poverty: A World Anti-Poverty Program in Outline*. New York: Pantheon, 1970.

For a Third World viewpoint see:

- Fanon, Frantz. *The Wretched of the Earth*, trans. Farrington. New York: Random House, 1968.
- Hensman, C.R. *Rich Against Poor: The Reality of Aid*. Hammondsworth, England: Penguin Press, 1971.

A good study of the role of multinational corporations in this problem will be found in:

* Barnet, Richard and Ronald Mueller. *Global Reach.* New York: Simon and Schuster, 1975.

Chapter Six deals with technology assessment and control. Lowe explores the need for a political economics capable of relating microdecisions to good macrodecisions. Hetman describes the characteristics of adequate technology assessment. Vickers deals with the fundamental problem of regulation, and Ferkiss identifies some of the characteristics of a paradigm capable of guiding our technological prowess:

* Lowe, Adolph. *On Economic Knowledge: Toward a Science of Political Economics.* New York: Harper and Row, 1965.
* Hetman, François. *Society and the Assessment of Technology.* Paris: Organization for Economic Cooperation and Development, 1973.
* Vickers, Geoffrey. *Freedom in a Rocking Boat: Changing Values in an Unstable Society.* Hammondsworth, England: Penguin Press, 1970.
* Ferkiss, Victor C. *Technological Man: The Myth and the Reality.* New York: Braziller, 1969.

For Chapter Seven the problem is selection—there are a multitude of sources, of varying quality. The chapter is essentially based on the SRI report *Changing Images of Man.* Foundation readings on the concept of image in social change will be found in Boulding and Polak:

* Markley, O.W. et al. *Changing Images of Man.* Menlo Park, California: Stanford Research Institute, May 1974.
* Boulding, Kenneth E. *The Image: Knowledge in Life and Society.* Ann Arbor: University of Michigan Press, 1961.
* Polak, Fred. *The Image of the Future,* trans. E. Boulding. San Francisco: Jossey-Bass, 1973.

Some characteristics of the emerging psychology are delineated in the following two works:

* Maslow, Abraham. *The Further Reaches of Human Nature.* New York: Viking Press, 1972.
* Bateson, Gregory. *Steps to an Ecology of Mind.* New York: Ballantine, 1973.

As to explorations of consciousness we shall content ourselves with four; references in those four will lead to other sources:

* Bucke, Maurice M. *Cosmic Consciousness: A Study in the Evolution of the Human Mind.* New York: Causeway Books, 1974 (original edition 1900).
* Huxley, Aldous. *The Perennial Philosophy.* New York: Harper and Brothers, 1945.
* Needleman, Jacob. *A Sense of the Cosmos: The Encounter Between Modern Science and Ancient Truth.* New York: Doubleday, 1975.
* Tart, Charles. *States of Consciousness.* New York: E.P. Dutton, 1975.

It is difficult to choose suitable introductory sources for the highly controversial area of psychic research, or parapsychology. I have selected Myers both for historical interest and because it is fascinating, Murphy because of the evaluation by an esteemed elder statesman of psychology, and Mitchell because of its being one of the most recent books:

* Myers, F.W.H. *Human Personality and its Survival of Bodily Death* (abridged). New Hyde Park, New York: University Books, 1961 (original edition 1903).
* Murphy, Gardner. *The Challenge of Psychical Research.* New York: Harper and Row, 1961.

- Mitchell, Edgar D. (John White, ed.). *Psychic Exploration: A Challenge for Science.* New York: Putnam, 1974.

Finally, relating to Chapters Eight and Nine, I have chosen eight quite varied books to mention. Hutchins deals with the "learning society" aspects of the future; Galbraith and Lodge with the economic and business aspects; Fromm and Roszak with psychological and cultural aspects. Martin's book provides a fascinating comparison of a half-dozen times in human history when it seemed that the ideal humane society was nearly within reach—optimistically raising the question of whether a new such vision has begun to appear. Fred Polak deals with the problem of social goals in an essay entitled "Towards the Goal of Goals," in the Jungk-Galtung collection. Thompson provides one man's overview of the whole contemporary scene.

- Hutchins, Robert. *The Learning Society.* New York: Praeger, 1968.
- Galbraith, John K. *Economics and the Public Purpose.* New York: Houghton-Mifflin, 1973.
- Lodge, George Cabot. *The New American Ideology.* New York: Knopf, 1975.
- Fromm, Erich. *The Revolution of Hope.* New York: Harper and Row, 1968.
- Roszak, Theodore. *Where the Wasteland Ends: Politics and Transcendence in Postindustrial Society.* New York: Doubleday, 1972.
- Martin, Malachi. *The New Castle: Reaching for the Ultimate.* New York: E.P. Dutton, 1974.
- Jungk, Robert and Johan Galtung, eds. *Mankind 2000.* London: Allen and Unwin, 1969.
- Thompson, William I. *At the Edge of History: Speculations on the Transformation of Culture.* New York: Harper and Row, 1971.

INDEX

Copernican, 34
French, 11
Industrial, 33–34
metanoia, 33
"in people's heads," 32
of rising expectations, 68
scientific, 34
Rise of the Meritocracy, The (Young), 113
Roman Empire, 117, 119
Rosicrucians, and perennial philosophy, 101, 105
Russia, 23

Saint-Exupéry, Antoine de, 97
St. Francis, 119
Science
  and consciousness exploration, 96–100, 109–110, 115
  legitimacy challenged, 81, 118
  as orthodoxy, 91–93
  supports self-realization ethic, 120
  technology depends on, 124
  testing knowledge in, 97, 98
  in transindustrial paradigm, 32–33, 123–124
Scientific determinism, 100
Scientific method, 24
Scientific paradigm, 95–96
  need to change, 142–143
  threatened, 96–98
Scientific revolution, 34
Self-acceptance, 105–106
Self-awareness, 32, 123. *See also* Awareness
Self-determination, 68
Self-knowledge, 98
Self-sufficiency, 47, 49
Skinner, B. F., 113
Slavery, 116, 125
Smith, Adam, 86, 111
Snow, C. P., 123
Social change
  alternatives to, 143–144
  and awareness, 5–7, 120, 141
  and concept of choice, 122–123
  disruption accompanying, 34, 35, 36. *See also* Social disorganization
  and energy use, 46–49, 84
  failures, 22
  in history, 21, 25, 33–34

  and images of man, 91
  indicators of, 28–29, 32
  and legitimacy challenge, 115–116, 117, 118
  matrix for whole-system, 136–141
  model for, 85–87
  need for, 10, 21–28
  and new paradigm, 28, 33–37
  resistance to, 144
  speed of, 37
  strategies for, 135–143
  and stress, 4–7
  and technology assessment, 81–83, 85, 87
  work roles and, 65
Social disorganization
  as advance sign of revolution, 117
  and distribution dilemma, 68
  and legitimacy challenge, 115–119, 135
  strategies for avoiding, 141–143
  and work-roles dilemma, 52, 53–54
Socialism, 27, 129
Social paradigm. *See* Paradigm
Social systems
  cause-effect relationships in, 13–14
  "central project" in, 56, 110, 111, 124
  challenging legitimacy of, 115–119, 135
  continuity in, 11–12, 17, 19, 107
  goal seeking in, 14
  holistic trending in, 14
  internal self-consistency in, 12, 17, 19
  need for guiding image of future, 114, 140–144 *passim*
  pluralism in, 2
  problems in remedying ills, 21–23
  resistance to change in, 144
  role of work in, 56–59, 60, 61
  self-realization ethic in, 120
  similarity among, 12–13
  stem from images of man, 91
  transindustrial, 126–131
  See also Western society
Social transformation. *See* Social change

morality challenged, 118
and multinational corporations, 85
suggestions for, 75–77, 139–140
See also Distribution, international
World War II
  aid to poor countries since, 74
  colonialism after, 116
  economic growth after, 41–42, 45
  freedom restricted during, 143

Yankelovich, Daniel, 29, 54, 147
Year 2000, The: A Framework for Speculation (Kahn & Wiener), 11
Yoga, 29, 32
Young, Michael, 113
Youth
  seek power, 116, 118
  in transindustrial society, 138, 139
  and employment, 51, 53, 54, 55

ABOUT THE AUTHOR

Willis Harman is director of the Center for Study of Social Policy at the Stanford Research Institute and professor of engineering-economic systems at Stanford. Professor Harman received his BS from the University of Washington and his PhD from Stanford.

A member of the Stanford faculty since 1949, he has written texts and papers on engineering, alternative futures, educational policy, and humanistic psychology. He was a Fulbright lecturer on communication theory at the Royal Technical University of Copenhagen and in 1958 was recipient of the George Washington Award from the American Society for Engineering Education for his outstanding contribution to engineering education.

For a period Professor Harman was active in the newly formed Association for Humanistic Psychology, serving as a member of the Executive Board and as a member of the Editorial Board of *The Journal of Humanistic Psychology.*

He entered the field of social policy analysis and in 1966 joined SRI, becoming director of the Educational Policy Research Center in 1967. In this work he has made various contributions to research on alternative futures and analysis of major societal problems. Harman has been a consultant to the National Goals Research Staff of The White House and to the Conference Board in New York. He is a member of the Commerce Technical Advisory Board serving the Department of Commerce.